THE
FACE
OF
RUSSIA

The Icon and the Axe:
An Interpretive History of Russian Culture

"This brilliantly written and comprehensive history of Russian culture, an artistic achievement in its own right, is a major contribution to Western understanding of the wellsprings of the Russian...spirit. Rarely is a great body of important information presented as charmingly and interestingly as Princeton's Professor Billington has succeeded in this work."   —*The New York Times*

"All in all, this thousand year cultural interpretation is a notable and ground-breaking achievement which has no parallel in American literature about Russia."
                                              —*Wall Street Journal*

"A rich and readable introduction to the whole sweep of Russian culture and intellectual history."
                                              —*Library Journal*

"Bold and brilliant."   —*Slavic Review*

Fire in the Minds of Men:
Origins of Revolutionary Faith

"A remarkable book, learned and lively, wide-ranging and probing, placing many aspects of revolutionary conviction and action in unaccustomed lights. Billington moves with assurance over the whole of modern history, at home in every decade and in a wide variety of countries."

—*New Republic*

"Billington describes revolutionary ideas, their sources and their development, and tells how they were transmitted over generations and across national boundaries....
He pays great attention to the lives and emotions of individuals, and this makes *Fire in the Minds of Men* absorbing."
—*The New Yorker*

Russia Transformed: Breakthrough to Hope, August 1991

"Billington, the Librarian of Congress and one of the foremost experts on Russian history, was in Moscow August 1991 during the failed Communist coup and the democratic counter-coup that swept Boris Yeltsin into power. In *Russia Transformed: Breakthrough to Hope*, a stirring, perceptive eyewitness account of the coup and its aftermath, he views these events as a decisive turning point that transformed the Russian people psychologically, forcing them to accept responsibility for moral choices."
—*Publishers Weekly*

"Billington is a rare and deeply erudite scholar of Russia who has based his approach on the unfashionable hunch that there is indeed such a thing as a Russian soul, and that the way to comprehend this vast and rich enigma of a country is to explore in the broadest sense its spiritual culture."
—*The Washington Post Book World*

THE
FACE
OF
RUSSIA

*Anguish, Aspiration,
and Achievement
in Russian Culture*

James H. Billington

New York

Publisher's Cataloging-in-Publication Data
Billington, James. H.
   The face of Russia: anguish, aspiration, and achievement in Russian culture / James H. Billington. — 1st ed.
      p. cm.
   Includes index.
   Companion volume to the PBS TV series: The face of Russia
   ISBN: 1-57500-089-X
   1. Russia—Civilization. 2. Russia (Federation)—Civilization. 3. Arts, Russian. 4. Russia—History. 5. National characteristics, Russian. I. Title.
   DK32.B55 1998   947
                                       QBI98-937

The publisher has made every effort to secure permission to reproduce copyrighted material and would like to apologize should there have been any errors or omissions.

The PBS series, "The Face of Russia," is a co-production of Malone Gill Productions and WETA Washington, D.C., with the participation of the U.S. Library of Congress, in association with Public Media Incorporated and Media-Most.

Videotapes of the three programs in the series, "The Face on the Firewood," "The Facade of Power," and "Facing the Future," are available individually or in a collectible boxed set through Home Vision Select. To order, call 1-800-826-FILM.

TV Books, L.L.C.
Publishers serving the television industry.
1619 Broadway, Ninth Floor
New York, NY 10019
www.tvbooks.com

Contents

THE
FACE
OF
RUSSIA

Preface

I composed this volume expanding on a PBS television series that I wrote and narrated under the same title. This book is designed for a broad readership and can be read independently or in conjunction with viewing the series, which is now available on video. It is organized into the same three parts as the series—and with the same five basic units treated in the same chronological order.

This book was written in the privacy of my home. The TV series was a collaborative undertaking in which the Library was a participant. I am indebted to my Library of Congress colleagues, Irene Steckler and Harry Leich, for their personal interest and expert advice on the book. I have been stimulated and enriched by colleagues in the film, music, photography, map and rare books divisions, as well as the European and Main Reading Room staffs.

The support of George Soros and his Open Society Foundation made the television series possible, which has enriched this book. I also appreciate the support of the other underwriters of the television series: Vladimir Gusinsky, whose independent television network NTV will carry the television series in Russia, Dresser Industries, the Archer Daniels Midland Corporation, CPB, PBS, and the Arthur Vining Davis Foundation. I also thank Sharon Rockefeller and Phyllis Geller of WETA in Washington, and the fine production team assembled for the TV series by Michael Gill. In particular, the series director Murray Gregor, associate producer Yelena Zagrevskaya, and chief cameraman Douglas Campbell each contributed to my thinking as well as to the production of the series during trips to Russia and Ukraine and subsequent editing sessions in London.

For the book, I owe special thanks to the Carnegie Corporation of New York and its past and present presidents, Drs. David Hamburg and Vartan Gregorian. Their support of my parallel project on the search for a post-Communist Russian identity has contributed importantly to this book.

My greatest substantive debt is to that last great embodiment of the pre-revolutionary culture of St. Petersburg and unparalleled student of Old Muscovy, Dmitry Likhachev. A series of long conversations with him, including an interview for this television series, has been in many ways a major source of inspiration—as have been my special mentors of earlier years, the late Georges Florovsky and Isaiah Berlin.

Among many whom I interviewed in depth for this series, I specially thank Naum Kleiman and Yury Norstein, both of whom graciously provided illustrations for this book, as well as Mstislav Rostropovich, who had been for me a special source of stimulus and inspiration during his Washington years. Among many other Russians, I owe special and continuous thanks to Ekaterina Genieva and V.V. Ivanov. I also appreciate the support given to the TV series by the past and present Russian Ministers of Culture, Evgeny Sidorov and Natalya Dementeva; the Deputy Minister of Culture, P.V. Khoroshilov; the director of the library program in the ministry, Evgeny Kuzmin; Mikhail Piotrovsky, director of the Hermitage Museum; the staff of the Tretyakov Gallery; and many other library and museum curators in Russia and Ukraine who have aided this project.

The Library of Congress's energetic and capable representative in Moscow, Mikhail Levner, has been particularly and continuously helpful. Special thanks for illustrations to Vladimir Gusev, Director of the Russian Museum, and William Brumfield, a distinguished historian and photographer of Russian architecture. Thanks also to Marina Serebriakova in Ferapontov and Nelly Belova in Vologda for their expert assistance in, and dedication to, those special centers of the Russian North. I also thank Declan Murphy, Dmitry Sidorov, Robert Dierker, George Borchardt, Father Boris Danilenko, and the many Russians over the years who have made the study of Russia such a rewarding personal experience.

I appreciate the enthusiasm and good counsel of the publisher Peter Kaufman, the editing of Keith Hollaman, and the fast production capabilities of TV Books which made it possible to write this book after the television series was completed. Needless to say, I alone am fully responsible for the content, the ideas, and whatever mistakes or shortcomings this work may be found to contain.

I feel a special debt to the Congress of the United States, a number of whose official delegations I have accompanied to Russia and many of whose members have encouraged me to produce a work something like this. The magnificent and unique collections in Russian and other foreign languages and cultures that Congress has encouraged its library to collect for nearly two centuries make the Library of Congress a singularly appropriate place to pursue projects like this—just as the quality and dedication of the remarkable staff that work here make it a continuing honor for me to be entrusted with leadership responsibilities.

I owe a great and continuing debt in all I do to the example of my brother David, to my departed friends Lon Horsey and Don Cadle, and—in more recent years—to Janet Chase and Barbara Sakamoto. I am particularly indebted to Caron Cadle Remshardt for her meticulous proofreading and editing of this work. All our family is especially grateful for the supportive friendship of Caron and her mother, Inge Cadle.

My deepest debt is to my beloved wife, Marjorie, and to my children, who have endured with good humor my long fascination and frequent time abroad dealing with Russia over many years. I affectionately dedicate this modest work to our 11 young grandchildren: Becky, Luke, Kent, Charlie, Jim, Duncan, Kate, Adam, Sarah, Nelson, and Jonathan. They have been the special joy of the years in which this project was conceived and finished.

James H. Billington
McLean, Virginia

Introduction

This is the story of the Russian people as seen through their art. It is a distinctive chapter in humanity's continuing quest to find meaning in life through creations that endure. It is the particular tale of a remarkable people who arrived relatively late on the stage of history. Yet in the course of the second Christian millennium, they rose out of obscure origins and inhospitable surroundings to build the largest land empire of all time and one of the world's great cultures.

Russian history is usually told in terms of how this people concentrated power and extended it beyond preexisting boundaries. The story is told here, rather, in terms of how they created art and drove it beyond previous limits. This is a story not of cumulative, evolutionary achievements, but of unpredictable outbursts—flash fires in endless snow, sensational creativity amidst senseless suffering.

Artistic creativity came later to Russia than to other great civilizations on the more temperate periphery of Eurasia. Russians produced "a culture of explosion" which periodically, almost volcanically, seemed to thrust up artistic mountain peaks directly from the unending steppe at the heart of the world's greatest landmass.

Peaks are easier to survey without surrounding foothills; and this history will focus on five peaks that successively rose up from the flat plain of ordinary Russian life. Russian artists repeatedly sought to relieve the monotony of what actually was (in Russian *byt*) by promoting new visions of what might be (in Russian *mozhet-byt*). But their reach usually exceeded their grasp. Russia's story—like many of its greatest artistic projects—is not complete; and the ending is still unknown.

For eight hundred years Russia's chronicle of aspiration was told mutely through pictures and buildings. Then, in the 19th century, it was written down in a language that people could read, and then lifted up into music that people could sing. Finally, in the 20th century, it was projected out through movies that everyone could enjoy— even in the midst of convulsive changes that no one could understand.

This story covers each of these five successive periods. In each age an essentially new art form burst onto the Russian scene, dealt with a central problem of the age, and produced an innovative pioneer. First came the medieval painter Andrei Rublev, then the early modern architect Bartolomeo Rastrelli, the early-19th-century writer Nicholas Gogol, the late-19th-century composer Modest Musorgsky, and, finally, the 20th-century filmmaker Sergei Eisenstein.

The overall story is easy to tell, but hard to believe. In each of these five periods Russians developed a new art form through a process that tended to pass through three implausible stages—each one seeming to contradict the one that went before.

First, and without much warning, these seemingly proud and self-centered people suddenly take over some new type of creative enterprise lock, stock, and barrel from precisely that more advanced foreign civilization which they had previously reviled. Second, having taken over in

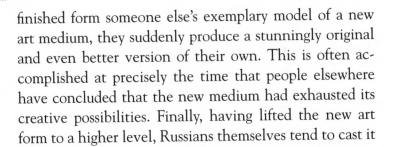

finished form someone else's exemplary model of a new
art medium, they suddenly produce a stunningly original
and even better version of their own. This is often accomplished at precisely the time that people elsewhere
have concluded that the new medium had exhausted its
creative possibilities. Finally, having lifted the new art
form to a higher level, Russians themselves tend to cast it
down and break it apart—leaving behind only fragments
of their best creations for future generations.

Does their past pattern of creativity provide any hints
at how Russians might solve their present problems? Having now borrowed the open democratic model of their
erstwhile American enemy, will they be able to create a
distinctive Russian variant that can endure? Or will they
end up destroying their own experiment at accountable,
constitutional government and returning to their long
tradition of authoritarianism?

The history of Russian culture provides no assurance,
but gives some grounds for hope. The Soviet empire was
finally overthrown by the Russians themselves in
Moscow, the very heart of Russia, in August 1991, thanks
largely to the resurfacing of moral forces deeply embedded
within Russian culture. This great change was more
nearly anticipated by humanistic students of creativity
than by economic and political scientists surrounded by
statistics and information.

Russians have faced "times of trouble" and crises of authority before in the course of their long history. Once legitimacy is reestablished, Russians have often not just reasserted their power, but extended their creativity into
new arenas with unexpected speed.

Whatever this story of breakdowns and breakthroughs

may tell us about the Russians, it should tell us something about artistic creativity. The unexpected suddenness of both accomplishment and destruction in Russia sometimes lays bare the heart of the artist—which often lies hidden within the body of more peaceful cultures.

Every human creation is unique. A structure can be best analyzed scientifically when an exact model is subjected to extreme stress which finally breaks it up into pieces. Artistic creativity may also be understood in new ways when stressed beyond the breaking point. Russians often seem to seek salvation more than satisfaction in their art; and artists can break under the weight of such expectation. Russian artists frequently leave behind only fractions of megalomanic projects that they either break up themselves or never come close to finishing.

The full story of Russian culture is what their people have done—and will do—with the pieces. At many points in this century it has seemed that only scattered scraps of their rich legacy have survived all the aggression from without, self-destruction from within, and rudderless freedom of recent years. But history is still open-ended—particularly for people that have often created best when troubles seemed worst and recovered their voice only after long silence.

It has been said that our only real crystal ball is a rearview mirror. Perhaps the Russians—and even we Americans—might be able better to put things together at the dawn of the coming millennium by casting a sympathetic backward glance at the anguish, aspirations, and achievements of the people that we looked on for so long as our adversary at the end of this last millennium.

PART I

THE MONKS

Among the great world civilizations, only that of the United States is younger than that of Russia. And the culture that grew up in Russia—like that of North America—was shaped by hardship and religion. Particularly difficult material conditions in Russia produced an unusually intense spirituality.

The unprotected interior steppe of the world's greatest landmass, Eurasia, edged north into dark forests and a virtual wasteland of scrub pine known as the *taiga*. Intense cold seems to have produced a compensating warmth in communal, human relations; and the relentlessly horizontal plain seems to have intensified the individual's longing to find a vertical link with God and some higher plane of reality.

By the time Russia acquired any clear cultural and political identity at the end of the 10th century A.D., the civilizations of Confucian East Asia and of the Indian subcontinent had long since mellowed into maturity; the great civilizations of classical antiquity had all risen and fallen long ago—in West Asia (Mesopotamia), North Africa (Egypt), and Europe (the Roman Empire). At the beginning of the second Christian millennium, a new Islamic Arab civilization reigned supreme in North Africa and the Middle East. And the Christian world was breaking apart into a western Europe that was politically divided and culturally backward but owed common allegiance to the Pope in Rome, and an Orthodox Byzantine Empire in the East.

Byzantium had been weakened by Islam but still preserved the vision that the Roman Empire survived in the Greek world even after it had collapsed in the Latin West in the fifth century. Constantinople (now Istanbul) was the "new Rome," the capital city of the Christian East, located on the straits that separate Europe from Asia in what is now Turkey. It was known to the early Slavs as "the city of the world's desire," and its main cathedral, Santa Sophia (Holy Wisdom), was the largest in Christendom.

Most of the vast heartland of Eurasia lacked any long-standing political authority or cultural identity. Nomadic peoples seemed to appear and disappear without a trace on the vast plain that stretched east from Germany to the Pacific and lay north of the fertile lands adjoining the Mediterranean, Black, and Caspian seas and of the desert sands of Central Asia and Mongolia. The region was as yet more a fact of geography than a factor in history. It was a world in which contending tribes and relatively primitive mini-nations lived in a constant state of armed truce—periodically invading more settled and civilized regions.

The savage Scythians swept in to dominate the region in the eighth century B.C., the Sarmatians in the third century B.C., the Goths at the beginning of the second century A.D., and the Huns at the end of the fourth century A.D. This pushed other tribes further west and south into the famed "Barbarian invasions" that led to the fall of Rome in the fifth century A.D. Almost nothing has survived from these transient realms except the hauntingly beautiful Iranian-Greek gold miniature jewelry of the Sarmatian period (the famed "Scythian gold" from southern Russia now kept in the Hermitage Museum in St. Petersburg)—and the recurring temptation for Russians to think of themselves as a uniquely "Eurasian" people who somehow belong neither to Europe nor to Asia.

It was one of these barbarian invasions that gave the Slavic population on that exposed eastern frontier of Europe its first government. The same Vikings whose violent incursions were shaking up western Europe in the ninth century appear to have made a more peaceful and commercial penetration of the steppe to connect the Baltic with the Mediterranean through the rivers of the Russian and Ukrainian plain.

According to the original sourcebook for Russian history, the so-called *Primary Chronicle*, written in the early 12th century, the Eastern Slavs on the steppe asked the Varangian (Viking) Prince Rurik to assume power in Novgorod on an eastern tributary of the Baltic Sea in 862 because "Our vast land is great and rich but there is no order here. Come and rule over us." The princely descendants of Rurik rapidly consolidated their rule over a series of Slavic cities along the rivers leading south to more established centers of civilization—and made the great cosmopolitan city of Kiev on the Dnieper River the site for their rule.

One of the great constants of Russian history—the desire for a strong, central authority—is thus affirmed in this, the very first account of that history. But the main focus of this early chronicle is on the other great constant of the Russian experience: the spirituality of its people. For the chronicle was written by a Monk Nestor, and it chiefly focuses on the gradual conversion to Byzantine Christianity by the heirs of the legendary Rurik—climaxing in the baptism of Prince Vladimir in 988 A.D. and the massive replacement of pagan idols in Kiev with the faith and culture of Eastern Orthodox Christianity.

It was—as we shall see—the beauty of Orthodoxy's pictorial theology and of its multi-medial worship services that converted Vladimir and the Eastern Slavs and made the Kievan realm devoutly Christian well before the other pagan peoples of Northern Europe. Spirituality and art were combined from the beginning in the new culture that emerged; the word "holy" was almost always associated with the term *Rus*, which was used to describe this new civilization. Art came suddenly as a finished product from the Byzantine Empire; and it was in the service of a higher calling.

Rus took over the finished product of Greek Christendom without much of the secular and critical heritage of classical Greece. Their literature no less than their liturgy was written in the new Slavic alphabet invented in the previous century by Byzantine missionaries from the Balkans, Cyril and Methodius. Rus was from the beginning a religious culture with its own language and a special sense of its own destiny. They were the first Byzantine converts from a region totally beyond the confines of the Old Roman Empire and a kind of divine compensation to the Orthodox world for the recent loss to Islam of the original sees of Christendom in the Holy Lands. Russians were the converts of the eleventh hour, inclined to believe that the end of time and the Last Judgment might not be far away.

The soaring spirituality and sense of destiny that became a hallmark of Russian culture was from the beginning tested and tempered by suffering. Divisions from within and invasions from without never seemed to cease from the very beginning of Russian and Ukrainian history. The major epic poem of Kievan Rus, *The Lay of the Host of Igor*, recounted one of the many continuing battles fought with the adjacent steppe people. Within a century of Vladimir's conversion the unity of Rus had broken up; in the 13th century Kiev was sacked by the Mongols and almost all of Rus plunged into a vassalage that lasted until the late 15th century.

The center of power moved north from the plain into the forest, from Kiev to the new capital of Moscow. Rus became Great Russia, which extended its imperial sway north to the Arctic and east to the Pacific by the late 17th century. But, in the process, the Russian Orthodox Church was rent by schism, the peasantry was brutally enserfed, and the social fabric was repeatedly torn apart by violent internal rebellion. All these horrors were magnified by the fires, famines, and plagues that were endemic in the wooden world of Muscovite Russia.

Suffering was interpreted biblically as divine chastisement and a call to repentance and renewed faith for a chosen people. Spirituality seemed to intensify with adversity; and closeness to nature seemed to strengthen Russians materially so that they could endure the extreme hardships on the eastern frontier of European civilization.

Russia's exposure to the West was both traumatic and transforming. When the hereditary line of rulers descended from Rurik died out in the late 16th century, Russia plunged into a "Time of Troubles": a chaotic crisis of legitimacy, marked by rebellion from below and invasion from without. There had been earlier Western incursions by the Teutonic knights in the 13th century, but the Polish invasion in the early 17th century led to the occupation of Moscow and the installation of a Polish pretender as Russian Tsar.

The Russians managed to turn back not only the

Polish invasion, but that of the Swedes at the beginning of the 18th century, the French at the beginning of the 19th, and the Germans twice in the 20th century. While outwardly fighting the leading military power of the West in each of these cases, the Russians were at the same time inwardly borrowing from these very adversaries—taking their modern governmental institutions from the Swedes, the language of the aristocracy from the French, and their basic forms of industrial organization from the Germans. In a sense, the Russians were simply following the precedent they had set by massively adopting the art and religion of Byzantium after opposing and occasionally raiding the Byzantine world for nearly a century.

Along with Russian Orthodox spirituality and closeness to nature, borrowing from the West became one of the three fundamental forces behind the development of Russian culture. Western borrowing became increasingly important in the modern era, because Russia was and remained a deeply split society internally. After the new capital of St. Petersburg was built on the westward-looking Baltic sea at the beginning of the 18th century, there were in effect three different Russias: the old rural and monastic culture still centered on the former capital of Moscow; the Old Believer communities that withdrew into the deep interior of Russia to avoid corrupting contact with either church or state; and the urbanized and secularized culture of the privileged aristocracy and imperial bureaucracy. Meanwhile, Kiev, the original capital of Rus, had become the center of a more Westernized Ukraine. The new Kyiv was uneasily reabsorbed into the Great Russian empire in 1667 and Ukraine redefined as "Little Russia."

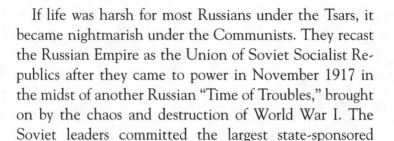

If life was harsh for most Russians under the Tsars, it became nightmarish under the Communists. They recast the Russian Empire as the Union of Soviet Socialist Republics after they came to power in November 1917 in the midst of another Russian "Time of Troubles," brought on by the chaos and destruction of World War I. The Soviet leaders committed the largest state-sponsored genocide of their own people in human history through purges, forced repopulation and starvation, particularly in Ukraine. The Communists created an unprecedented internal empire of gulags or slave labor camps.

Despite untold suffering within their land, the Russian people rose up to repel Hitler in World War II. This victory was achieved at immense human cost which, paradoxically, relegitimized the Soviet regime and helped it to survive essentially unchanged and toying with further imperial adventures for another 40 years.

If totalitarianism had no real precedent in human history, neither did its final collapse in Moscow in August 1991. Faced with a final Communist putsch, Russia destroyed the Soviet Union in a way that was as non-violent and decisive as it was unexpected and unplanned. But, once again, there was to be new human suffering and dislocation amidst the sudden imperial collapse, social chaos, and precipitous decline in living standards of early capitalism.

As the new Russia felt its way towards creating an accountable and participatory government and a more open society, it tended once again to borrow from the power that had been its principal Western adversary: the United States. As they struggled to build a new, post–Cold War culture in freedom, Russians sought, however, not just to replicate the material accomplishments of the West, but also to recover their own historic spirituality that had been nearly wiped out by the world's first atheistic state.

As Russians rediscovered the fullness of their cultural past in the midst of a new crisis of political legitimacy and "Time of Troubles," they found three buried layers—each of which had been superimposed on the others without ever fully replacing them. The top and most visible layer was the emerging mass culture of the late 19th century with its rich literature and music and its politicized intelligentsia; beneath it lay the imperial culture of the 18th century with its magnificent architecture centered in St. Petersburg and its court aristocracy; and at the base of it all was the original Orthodox culture of the Eastern Slavs, centered now more on Moscow than on Kiev and created by Russia's first and most long-lasting cultural elite: the monks.

The monastic artists properly begin our story; for these celibate holy men created an original, Christian culture that was sustained with remarkably few changes into the mid-17th century—carrying a medieval world view far deeper into modern Russia than into any other European state. Monks created the lasting presumption that art was a means to the end of salvation rather than an end in itself. Art was to prepare people for the Last Judgment rather than for the next amusement.

If the monks in early Kievan Rus took over Byzantine Orthodoxy lock, stock, and barrel from Byzantium in its prime, later monks around Moscow created an innovative, more humanized variant of that Byzantine heritage by intensifying both inner spirituality and a sense of linkage with nature and the local community. Finally,

the holy men of old Russia divided into two camps which fatally split the church and much of Russian society in the second half of the 17th century. In slow motion, the pictorial monastic culture of Old Russia went through a cultural cycle of borrowing, innovating and destroying new art forms—a cycle that would be repeated on a faster timetable in the later Russian reception of other art media.

Even in its periods of decline and near extinction in the 18th and again in the 20th centuries, the monastic culture spun off a penumbra of holy fools and wandering prophets who continued to frighten the powerful and fascinate the rebellious. Indeed, underlying most of the entire millennium of Russia's existence as a distinct civilization is the continuous tension between power and truth, the material drive to expand out and the spiritual search to go deeper within. It may be, in the last analysis, that Russia has been able to overcome all its suffering and extrude all foreign invaders—even including ultimately the alien ideology of Marxist Communism—because of the inner strength that comes from the unspoken but widespread belief that Russia is defined, at its core, by the integrity of its internal life more than by the extent of its external power.

We can never penetrate fully into the internal world of silence and unending worship that was—and still is—the monastic life in Russia. But the monks left us a trail of chapels and churches on the path they blazed north to the Arctic and then east to the Pacific. The way was long and hard, but the journey was seen as preparation for their future passage from earth to heaven. Painting provided the outward and visible signs of their inner and spiritual grace; and the coming of culture to the forbidding eastern frontier of Europe properly begins with the story of holy pictures in Russia and of the monks who made them and were at times depicted on them.

Chapter 1

The Face
on the Firewood:
The Painting of Rublev

O f all the arts, icon painting was the first that Russians
   made their own. In the first century of the second
Christian millennium, they suddenly and uncritically
adopted the pictorial Christianity of Byzantium. In the
middle of the millennium they produced their own stunningly original version. In the last century of the millennium, they almost obliterated it all.

Who are these people who borrow so totally, innovate
so radically, destroy so cruelly? We in the West hardly got
to know them in the long Cold War years as we stared at
the face of power. We now face a people embarked on a
new course with no assured destination. It may be time to
look for the human face revealed in their art—and at
their recurrent tendency to take over, lift up, and then
cast down new forms of creativity. The all-important
question for Russians today is whether they will eventually lift up or cast down their present efforts to master the
art of constitutional self-government.

Holy pictures gave a human face to the new faith of the

Russians. We now know that Old Russia was a more ethnically diverse civilization than often thought, having absorbed many elements from other steppe peoples. So it was holy pictures rather than anthropological characteristics that first gave a unifying identity to the Russians.

Andrei Rublev, the greatest of all icon painters, painted a Christ in the early 15th century that was unlike any previous depiction in Christian art (see illustration 1). The face was elongated, as if to flow with the grain of the wood on which it was painted. The austere and hitherto sacrosanct Byzantine model was softened by abstraction suggestive of the image of the preceding pagan protector of hearth and home: the *domovoi*. Rublev's Christ is recognizably human, but not of this world. He is looking out, but not at us. Large eyes over a small mouth both suggest and invite contemplation, not conversation.

Rublev's painting was the creation of a monk and the expression of a monastic ideal that helped unify all the people of an otherwise divided, diverse, and dispersed civilization. The painting was designed for a new church serving the general population in the relatively new town of Zvenigorod. It was the central panel in a multitiered screen of icons, known as an *ikonostas*. This composite pictorial encyclopedia of faith was itself a recent Russian innovation, providing a largely illiterate populace with a focus for both instruction and veneration.

We know almost nothing for certain about Rublev except that he was already a monk in 1405 and had for a long time been working with a team that was headed by a Greek master painter named Theophanes. Andrei of Crete was his patron saint; and it seems stylistically likely that he worked with and was influenced by not only

Greek, but also South Slav monks fleeing the Orthodox kingdoms of Serbia and Bulgaria, which were being over-run (as Constantinople itself was to be in 1453) by the Muslim Turks. Rublev was creating paintings of great serenity in and around Moscow at a time of increased conflict with Eastern enemies. The Russians had for the first time defeated the Mongols in a major battle at Ku-likovo on the Don River in 1380 only to see Tamerlane lead a fresh band of Eastern invaders to the gates of Moscow in the 1390s. The beauty and calm of Rublev's creations helped compensate for the ugliness and agitation unfolding all about him.

Rublev's great icon from Zvenigorod is simply called *Spas*, the Savior. The Christ at the center of a Russian icon screen was not a teacher but a Savior; not the author of a doctrine, but the hero of a story—the ongoing story of God bringing salvation to humanity. The saga worked its way down the icon screen from large panels on the top row depicting Old Testament Kings, through a row of prophets, to the "prayer row" depicting the New Testa-ment company of Christ, down finally to ground level where icons of local saints and current feasts brought the story up to date and into the lives of the congregation.

The typical Savior at the center of a Russian icon screen faced the congregation from a throne holding a Bible opened to the gospel passage "Come unto me all you who travail and are heavy laden, and I will refresh you." A believer, meditating on the beauty and order of an icon screen inside a church, often found not merely re-freshment, but compensation for the ugliness and disor-der of life outside on the cold and unprotected eastern frontier of Europe.

Rublev's Christ lacks a full body, hands, or Bible. We find ourselves face-to-face with nothing but his face. It is the first—and in many ways the most enduring—face of Russia.

But it was a face on firewood—discarded and almost incinerated—like the faith itself—amidst the terrors of the 20th century.

Only the Spas and two other panels from Rublev's Zvenigorod screen have survived into modern times. Most great icons were lost, burnt, or covered with either the soot of worshipers' candles or the inferior overpainting of misguided modernizers. In the cold winter of 1918 in newly Communist Russia, Rublev's Christ was thrown into a woodpile and earmarked to be burned. It was saved from the furnace and taken to Moscow; but almost everyone who publicly championed the preservation of icons in the early Soviet period was later murdered in the 1930s during the most extensive persecution of Christians in modern times.

Credit for the rescue of Rublev's Christ (and of his equally sublime icons of St. Paul and the Archangel Michael) is still generally given to Communist-supported art historians. But some say that the face on the firewood was first pulled out of the woodpile by a local priest who later died in the Stalinist repression. Whether this particular tale is true or not, there is little doubt that anonymous and often heroic believers did more quietly to save Russia's treasury of icons from total destruction than did the second thoughts and pompously self-congratulatory token efforts of the post-Stalinist Soviet cultural bureaucracy.

Icons are now being returned to churches and painted anew in many parts of post-Communist Russia. Disillusioned both with the systematic lies of the official written culture of the Soviet era and with the emptiness of atheist ideology, many Russians are now tired of talk—and willing to look anew at pictures that provide windows into another, purer world.

What is the origin of the early Russian passion for seeking a link with the eternal through pictures rather than words? The answer to this—as to so many mysteries—may well lie in the sands of Egypt: among a people whose words were pictures.

The ancient pictorial language of Egyptian hieroglyphics had focused for centuries on attempting to chart the mysterious journey that we all must take from this world to the next. The path was littered with pictures of half-animals, animals and even insects. The last earthly stop was the tomb containing the mummified body of the royal leader who, having completed the journey, was crowned with a majestic mask placed over his face.

We will never know all the secrets of the Egyptian tombs. But the Pharaoh's mask seemed to represent the ideal image that he was taking into the next world. Three thousand years of this mysterious funerary art came to an end when first the Greeks and then the Romans conquered the land of the Pharaohs. But the new culture seemed to want something similar for its own dead. So Hellenistic artists created a variant that showcased their own, more naturalistic style of painting.

Like the Pharaohs before them, the new leaders of Egypt were mummified with ideal images placed over their faces. But their artists flattened the old death masks and made them more human.

The new burial masks were classical portraits of the late Roman Empire; and a large number of those painted between the first and fourth centuries A.D. were preserved in the large Fayum oasis some 50 miles west of the Nile and south of the pyramids.

The encaustic technique used in the Fayum paintings (fixing bright colors with burnt wax and egg-based tempera paint on wooden panels) seems to have been taken over by some of the early monks and martyrs of the Christian church, who fled into the unpopulated desert around Fayum to escape from urban decadence and Roman persecution.

The original desert fathers of Christianity seem to have adopted this idea of painting the ideal image of a revered figure over his face at burial. These portraits served as portable reminders and objects of veneration during the believers' perpetual flights from imperial authorities.

Holy pictures began to proliferate throughout the eastern Mediterranean after the Emperor Constantine converted to Christianity at the beginning of the fourth century and built his "new Rome" of Constantinople. This city became the capital of the Byzantine or East Roman Empire which lasted a thousand years beyond the fall of Rome and of the Western Empire in the fifth century.

Constantine's new capital was built along the narrow strip of water that separates Europe from Asia and the Mediterranean from the Black Sea. Constantinople promoted its new-found religion with pictures—which were understandable to everyone within the polyglot Eastern Empire (and to equally venerable Christian

cultures in nearby Georgia and Armenia who also celebrated the faith with pictures hewn on rock or colored
into manuscripts).

The new Christian art of the Orthodox Empire grew
out of the preexisting mosaics, reliefs, and frescoes of classical antiquity. Christian artists added a whole new world
of subject matter, but, in painting their earliest holy pictures, they relied on the encaustic technique used at
Fayum of burning images with wax onto wooden panels.
Known by the Greek word for picture, *ikon*, these first
icons were, like the Fayum portraits, painted in a classical, almost lifelike style.

By the early eighth century, such Christian pictures
had come to seem too sensuous and pagan for a series of
puritanical emperors in Constantinople. They denounced
icons as graven images prohibited by the Second Com-
mandment; and, for more than a century, these original
"iconoclasts" set out to destroy them all. They would
have succeeded totally had not the desert once again
come to the rescue.

More than 200 of these early icons miraculously survived in the remote Monastery of St. Catherine's at the
foot of Mount Sinai, where the monks believed that
Moses received the Ten Commandments. The link between classical and Christian art, which had first been
forged by itinerant desert hermits on the Egyptian side
of the Red Sea, was saved by desert monks on the other
side. And it was in the often remote monasteries of the
Christian East that icon painting revived most spectac-
ularly after the fall of iconoclasm.

Of all the many victories over heresies in the early
church, only the one that restored icon veneration is for-

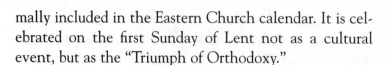

mally included in the Eastern Church calendar. It is celebrated on the first Sunday of Lent not as a cultural event, but as the "Triumph of Orthodoxy."

By the time iconoclasm was definitively rejected in 843, the original sees of Christendom in the Holy Lands and North Africa had been conquered by the new religion of Islam, which also prohibited the pictorial representation of sacred figures. Cut off from the south, Orthodox Christian missionaries turned north and took their art of holy painting into a succession of new monasteries in the South Slav kingdoms of Serbia and Bulgaria, on to the more Latinized Romanians, and, finally, to the less familiar peoples who lived beyond the farthest borders of the old Roman Empire on the vast inner plain of the Eurasian heartland. There, a conglomerate group of Eastern Slavs—the Russians, Ukrainians, and Belorussians of today—acquired a common cultural identity when Prince Vladimir of Kiev accepted Christianity from Constantinople in 988 A.D.

The pagan Eastern Slavs had been in many ways the wild men of eastern Europe. They had previously reviled—and even raided—Constantinople. But their capital city of Kiev was—like Constantinople itself—a large, ethnically diverse, and cosmopolitan city connected by water with the Black Sea. Located on a hill overlooking the steppe far up the Dnieper River, Kiev imported the resurgent pictorial Christianity of Constantinople deep into Eurasia and created a purely Byzantine city with the uncritical enthusiasm of new converts. Vladimir's son, Yaroslav the Wise, built a Cathedral of the Holy Wisdom filled with mosaics and frescoes in imitation of its namesake in Constantinople, then the largest church in Christendom. Yaroslav's long reign (1019–54) was a kind of golden age, which left Kiev—in the words of its first native church leader:

> a city glistening with the light of holy icons, fragrant with incense, ringing with praise and holy, heavenly songs.

Russian icon painting seems to have begun—like its Egyptian progenitor—as a funereal art. The first Russian icon painter, Alypius, worked and was buried in the subterranean catacombs under the main hill of Kiev. This was where Russia's earliest holy men were mummified and placed in niches along with a holy picture, their window into the next world, with uncovered hands placed over their hearts as a gesture of perpetual repentance.

These caves were the very heart of *Rus*—the name originally given to this new Orthodox Christian civilization. The word was almost always combined with " holy" or "mother" in later Russian usage. The Monastery of the Caves above the tombs was the first of the four great mother-monasteries of Rus (known as *lavras*) that combined solitary work and prayer with festal communal worship. Kiev itself, though located in Ukraine, was called "the mother of Russian cities."

The most revered icon in Russian history was a Byzantine image of the Mother of God that was brought to Kiev from Constantinople (see illustration 2) in order to provide the same divine protection for the Slavs that the Virgin was long believed to have given the Greeks. It shows a majestic woman extending her face down tenderly to the Christ child. When Kievan Rus began to fall apart well before being overrun by the Mongols in the early 13th century, this icon was taken north from the plain into the forest so that it—and Rus itself—could be saved.

This signature icon of Rus was taken from Kiev to the new capital of Vladimir, where it acquired the first and most enduring of its many names: the Vladimir Mother of God. The seat of princely power and its legitimating icon subsequently moved from Vladimir to neighboring Moscow. Like Vladimir, Moscow was located on a tributary of the great Volga River, which leads east into the Caspian Sea and Asia. In contrast, Kiev (like most of the original cities of Rus including Novgorod to the north) was on a body of water that flows west to Europe. These more westerly early centers of Rus generally maintained throughout the Mongol period the links with Europe that had characterized the Kievan golden age. This was the beginning of the more Western orientation that was to be characteristic of modern Ukraine or "Little Russia." A more isolated Great Russian civilization began slowly to emerge in the forested Vladimir-Moscow region to the north and east.

The central cathedrals in both Vladimir and Moscow were dedicated not to the Holy Wisdom as in Constantinople, Kiev and Novgorod, but to that most mysterious of all feasts to the Mother of God: the Assumption. The final entrance of Mary into heaven after her passing from earthly life meant that she was now reigning in heaven and interceding with God himself on behalf of the faithful still on earth. She provided, in a sense, the ultimate security policy for a people perpetually threatened both by nomadic invaders that came from the east to pillage and by raging fires that came out of nowhere to incinerate its cities.

In both Vladimir and Moscow, the icon of the Vladimir Mother of God was venerated inside a cathedral dedicated to the Assumption within the city's central citadel which was called a *kremlin*, from the Russian word for "strong place." The Cathedral of the Assumption within the Moscow Kremlin was to become the heart of the modern Russia that grew out of medieval Rus. It was the place both where Tsars were crowned and where Communist dictatorship was finally exorcised. The first Russian parliament not under Communist discipline was formally opened by a service in the Cathedral of the Assumption on the Feast of the Assumption on August 26, 1991.

Icons of the Madonna gave a sense of security not just in the centers of power but on the frontiers of faith. Particularly in the provinces, the model of the Vladimir Mother of God inspired many other variants of this type known as Our Lady of Tenderness.

Russians liked to see the Mother compassionately pressing her face against that of the child (always shown as a mature savior). Her visage often became larger than life; and the angle of her downward extension to her Son more extreme than was anatomically possible.

In Old Russia, some version of the Vladimir Mother of God was often the first icon shown to a newborn baby for protection. But the talismanic original was not able to save either Vladimir or Moscow from the invading Mongols who reduced most of Rus to dependency status for nearly 250 years.

The Mongols (or Tatars as the Russians generally

called them) swept across the steppe and sacked Kiev in 1240 under the leadership of the grandson of Genghiz Khan. With the fastest cavalry and best internal discipline and communication system ever seen, the Mongols burned and depopulated much of the Russian North as well—conducting the only successful winter invasion of Russia in all of history. The Mongol Khans were not defeated by Russian forces until the Battle of Kulikovo in 1380, but continued to exact monetary tribute from Moscow until 1480 and to occupy much of the southern steppe for many years thereafter.

The Mongols effectively cut Russia off from Byzantium and most of Europe, and created an authoritarian political model for the new Russian power center of Moscow, which gathered on the upper tributaries of the Volga the tribute that was paid to the Khans at their headquarters on the lower Volga. Many Russian words for weapons and money are Mongol in origin—as was the Russian practice of prostration before the monarch (the term for "petition" itself was "beating the forehead," *chelobitnaya*). Raids by successor Mongol mini-states continued periodically until the last of these, the Tatar Khanate of Crimea, was defeated and absorbed into the Russian Empire in 1783.

But the Orthodox Christian culture of Rus was left relatively untouched by the Mongols after the first, furious rampage of destruction in the mid-thirteenth century. In the distant and protected forest regions of the North, the city of Moscow slowly grew from being an almost unknown wooden village into the bastion of a resurgent civilization celebrated as the "white stone" site of "forty-forties" (1600 churches)—and the political base for expansion into the thinly populated regions to the north and east.

The Russian people's amazing push forward into some of the coldest regions of the world eventually encompassed 15 time zones. They extended the eastern frontier of European Christian civilization across Siberia to Alaska—and on to meet America's western frontier at the Russian outpost of Fort Ross just north of San Francisco in the early 19th century.

The Russians' constant companion in exploration, their banner in battle, their consolation in suffering was the icon. It was the understandable human image of the Lord they served, His Mother who protected them, the saints and martyrs who inspired them.

Rublev's icon of the Savior, our archetypical Face of Russia, was created in this period of Russian resurgence by a monk who appears to have spent almost all of his life in the late 14th to early 15th centuries painting holy pictures in and around Moscow. But all that is known for sure about Rublev from the chronicles of the time is that he worked with other monks including Theophanes "the Greek" and Daniel "the Black."

Religious painting in this explosively creative period was a deeply devotional, deliberately anonymous, communal activity. Each stage in the preparation of materials and in the painting of the icon was preceded by prayer. One monk sketched the lines, another filled in one set of colors, a third added another set, and yet another painted the pure white sometimes gilded with gold that was reserved not for saints, but for the direct presence of divinity in time—as in the dazzling image of Christ in icons of the Transfiguration (see illustration 3).

The sudden breakthrough by Rublev into an original, Russian school of painting was basically generated by a religious community 40 miles northeast of Moscow: the famed Monastery of the Holy Trinity. It had been newly hewn out of the virgin forest, and it illustrated even as it inspired the opening of the forest frontier of Great Russia.

This monastery was, at the outset, a kind of spiritual stockade that formed around (and was popularly named for) its founder, St. Sergius from the nearby forest village of Radonezh. He was idealized already in his lifetime as the model *podvizhnik* or "heroic mover" of an advancing Christian civilization and is depicted in Russian hagiography as a kind of combination of St. Francis and Paul Bunyan. The monastery centered on the white-stoned Trinity Cathedral, which rapidly became the second great mother monastery (*lavra*) of the Eastern Slavs and still today contains his venerated remains and relics.

The Monastery of St. Sergius and the Holy Trinity gave birth to a string of frontier monasteries that stretched far into the Arctic North—including the massive complexes of St. Cyril's on the White Lake in 1397, and Sts. Savva and Zosima on Solovetsk Island in the White Sea in 1436, just a century after the founding of St. Sergius's mother house. As the great lavra itself was transformed from wood into stone, it acquired the thickest walls in all Russia. Almost alone of all the major cultural centers within the confines of the original patrimony of Kievan Rus, the Monastery of St. Sergius and the Holy Trinity was never either captured by invaders from without or sacked by tyrants from within.

But Soviet Communism in the terrible decade of the

1930s tried systematically to destroy the church and closed the monastery, confiscating its library, and imprisoning or murdering most of its monks. This monastery almost alone in the early Soviet period had kept alive the scholarly study as well as the physical restoration and prayerful veneration of icons. It was totally deserted for 15 years until Stalin gave some limited rights to the church in 1943 in return for its all-out support of the war effort. In the post-war years, the lavra gradually recaptured its place as the principal center of teaching and worship in Russia.

Rublev painted his Spas at the request of the monk who succeeded Sergius as leader of the lavra. It was designed for yet another Cathedral of the Assumption, the first stone church in Zvenigorod. The same monastic leader later asked Rublev to paint his icon of the Trinity for the lavra itself.

When Communism came, these and other important icons were taken to Moscow—but were kept out of sight and only intermittently edged back into public view in the later Soviet period. Beginning in 1964, however, with the first summer expedition of 500 Moscow students out into the countryside to recover icons, the faces on firewood became a source and symbol of Russian determination to recover its past and to discover a future beyond Communism. Icons were, quite simply, too small and numerous and widely distributed all over Russia to be as easily and totally destroyed as were the monks who painted them and the churches that housed them.

Symbolic of the rise, fall, and resurrection of Russian Orthodox culture was the fate of the last great church ever built in Moscow and the largest in all Russian history: the Church of Christ the Savior. Designed as a memorial to the Russian victory over the Napoleonic invaders with a dome higher than St. Peter's in Rome, it took 34 years to build in the mid-19th century, but only a few minutes to blow up entirely in December 1931; and then, again, only a few months to rebuild meticulously in the mid-1990s after the fall of Communism.

By that time, thousands of churches that had been converted to profane uses all over Russia during the Soviet era were being returned to believers. Church bells were being rung and icons hung once more in the buildings for which they were designed.

Bells, like icons, in Russia had a certain affinity with the spirituality of the non-Christian East that was not to be found in the West. An icon, like a Buddhist image, conveyed its spiritual mood in significant part by the hands and face—usually the only flesh made visible in an icon and the only part never covered with metal adornments. A Russian bell was rung from the inside as in the West. But, as in the Buddhist East, it was immovable and thought to radiate its sanctity out as far as its sound could be heard.

The booming sonority of Russian bells, like the growing monumentality of Russian icon screens and frescoes in the 15th and 16th centuries, lent a certain solemnity and even megalomania to the culture that radiated out from Moscow. Both bell and icon were increasingly used to sanctify the authority that was being consolidated inside the Kremlin by the princes who came to call themselves Tsars, the Russian version of Caesar, after the "new Rome" of Constantinople fell to the Muslim Turks in 1453. The niece of the last Byzantine emperor married

Ivan III 19 years later, lending genealogical credibility to the idea of Moscow as the "third Rome." Perhaps the two most imposing creations within the Moscow Kremlin became then—and have remained ever since—the bell tower of Ivan III ("the Great") and the sea of holy pictures intermixing princes, warriors, and saints that covers the entire interior of the Cathedral of the Assumption.

But how could a faith focused on icons for monastic meditation energize the clearing of a frontier and forging of an empire? The answer lies hidden in the Russians' own version of the desert—the place in which icons had been created in the first place.

The typical monastic settlement through which Russians extended their frontier into the wilderness was called a *pustyn*, the Russian word for "desert." And a typical lonely hermitage located still further out for individual spiritual purification was a *skit*, meaning "place of wandering." Unlike many holy men in other eastern lands, pioneering Russian monks were not seeking mystical union with the "essence" of God. Rather, they were seeking a connection with what they called His "energies." Both monastic and secular pioneers sought to become movers, *podvizhniki*.

But motion came out of silence. Muscovy was under the sway of a meditative tradition generated by monks in the great Greek monastic complex on the rugged peninsula of Mount Athos during the late years of the Byzantine Empire. Known as *hesychasm* (from the Greek word for silence), this movement taught that a monk should struggle for purification not to avoid sin but to safeguard prayer.

Russians generally prayed with their eyes not closed, but open—and fixed on an icon. Praying was "meditating in colors," and if a monk could pray continuously with his whole body and soul, he might himself become a spiritually translucent figure through whom the divine light might shine for others. On the way to becoming a saint (for which the Russian word was *sviatoi*, meaning "light"), the monk had to become a kind of living icon. A person who had attained this level of sanctity was called *prepodobny*, or "very like" the dematerialized figures in holy paintings. After long silence in the desert, God's grace might bestow the gift of being able to "speak only in a state of sweetness." A young apprentice in this purifying adventure was called a *poslushniik*, "an obedient listener." He had listened above all to a *starets*, or "elder," who had attained this higher state and was thus able to serve as a "spiritual father."

The monastic artist closest to Rublev was Theophanes the Greek, who crystallized the hesychast ideal in a dematerialized, dazzlingly white, almost abstract fresco of St. Macarius, the fourth-century Egyptian ascetic who had spent 60 years in the Egyptian desert (see illustration 4). Theophanes painted this and a host of such images for Novgorod's Church of the Transfiguration, and later painted one of the most stunning icons ever crafted of the moment when Christ first appeared to his disciples in a transfigured state on Mount Tabor even before his passion and death on the cross (see illustration 3). The Transfiguration was central to the hesychast vision that purified men might themselves attain a measure of divine translucence even on earth—and actually become, as well as create, something of celestial beauty that could help transform the ugliness of ordinary life.

"Beauty will save the world," said Prince Myshkin, the modern Christ figure in Dostoevsky's *Idiot*. Orthodox Christians believe that all essential doctrines were resolved by the first seven Ecumenical Councils of the Church. The Second Council of Nicaea (the last of the seven) justified the return of icons by the fact that God had sent his son into a fallen world and restored man's "soiled image to its former state, suffusing it with divine beauty." It was the beauty of Byzantine Christianity that converted the Eastern Slavs when they went religion shopping in the 10th century and discovered in Constantinople that

> we did not know whether we were in heaven or earth. For on earth there is no such splendor or beauty, and we are at a loss to describe it. We know only that God dwells here among men and that their worship is more beautiful than that of other nations; we cannot forget that beauty.

Since all doctrinal questions had long ago been resolved by the Church fathers, the appropriate task remaining was to beautify rather than analyze the faith. And Rublev took beauty to an altogether new level in his last great icon, the Holy Trinity, painted in memory of St. Sergius.

Icons relate stories, not theories. They could depict only what people actually saw. Thus, a mystery like the Trinity was represented by its historical foreshadowing in the Book of Genesis by the three angels who visited

Sarah and Abraham. They are human, not allegorical figures, but appear in transfigured form—divested, as it
were, of their earthly bodies (see illustration 5).

Unlike the perspective found in Western paintings
which draw us into a disappearing point within the picture, austerely two-dimensional Russian icons have an
"inverse perspective" that thrusts focal points out at us,
reminding us of our distance from heavenly things. Unlike earlier icon painters, Rublev eliminates the figures of
Sarah and Abraham and any depiction of the food being
fed the angels. By clearing out and simplifying the composition Rublev helps us to contemplate without distrac-
tion the mysterious harmony of the three angels.

The central angel points to the key object and focal
point of the picture: the communion elements through
which an imperfect humanity finds its link with the angelic
community, the communion of saints. Russians had developed through all their ordeals a strong sense of community.
Their word for cathedral, sobor, also means "gathering" and
"council"—and suggests "togetherness." The sinuous lines
and deep colors of the angels symbolizing the three persons
of the Trinity seem harmoniously interrelated. And the
overall unity and harmony of the composition suggests
through sight something that could never be proven
through speech: that the three persons within God's own
nature represent the ultimate model of community.

For the early church fathers, God was "the most paradoxical of all things. For in him stability and movement
are the same thing." Medieval mystics believed that man
could find inner peace and stability by the silent contemplation of three equal and intersecting circles. That is the
essence of the composition Rublev used in his last great

painting, the highest achievement of pictorial Christianity in the medieval East.

As if by providential design, Dante had drawn on the same image a few years earlier at the very end of his *Divine Comedy*, the high point of literary Christianity in the medieval West. They could never have known of each other, but Dante seems almost to be providing a poetic meditation on the painter's vision:

> In the profound and shining being of a deep light
> There appeared to me three circles—
> Three colors, but one continuity...
> I saw how the image consorts with the circle
> And how it wove into unity...
> At this high fantasy all power failed.
> But already desire and will were rolled—
> Like a wheel moving in perfect stability—
> By love which moves the sun and all the stars.

Holy paintings did not just lift man's gaze to heaven; they also brought divine things down to earth. As Christian art moved into the Russian interior it necessarily absorbed elements from the preexisting pagan polytheism.

The Russians' distinctive stress on the maternity more than the virginity of Mary was intensified by memories of a prior belief in the Damp Mother Earth. The preexisting gods sometimes continued to be worshiped even by Christians: a phenomenon Russians call *dvoeverie* or duality of belief. The pagan god of thunder often blended into the image of the prophet Elijah; the *domovoi*, protector of households, into St. Paraskeva.

The White Horse—symbol of the Sun God long

revered in dark northern climates—reappeared as the dominant figure in Russian icons of the dragon-slaying St. George and of the martyrs Florus and Laurus. A sun was sometimes painted on Saint George's shield, and the horse's shape distorted to suggest its solar significance (see illustration 6).

The gilded, onion-shaped dome that replaced the Byzantine hemisphere atop churches in the Russian North was itself seen as a "sun," and the greatest of all Russian wooden churches, the 22-domed Church of the Transfiguration at Kizhi, may have been built on the site of a pre-existing shrine to the Sun God. It was coated with 30,000 shingles and put together without nails. Its low interior ceiling was covered with a sea of holy pictures called a "sky" and centered on a "sun" (Christ) who radiated out rays of sanctity that were in fact elongated, triangular icons of saints (see illustrations 7 and 8).

This church is located on an island in the often treacherous Lake Onega. Water transportation was so important on the often interconnected wide rivers and lakes of the Russian interior that navigators often sculpted images of the sun on the prow of their ships. Icons of St. Nicholas, the patron saint of travellers, showed him miraculously rescuing ships and were specially venerated.

Pilgrims generally approached a monastery across a body of water (a symbolic purification) and entered the "Jordan gate" through which the priest came to bless the waters at Epiphany.

As wooden churches were replaced by stone within the monasteries, holy painting spilled out from the icon screen to cover the entire interior. And there may be no more miraculous profusion of religious painting in all of

Christendom than the universe of frescoes which the monk Dionysius created for the Cathedral of the Nativity of the Virgin in distant Ferapontov in an astonishingly short time, between August 6 and September 8, 1502. Mary's birth is depicted in exterior frescoes over the door. The story is on the outside. But the glory lies within.

The interior of this recently restored church is, quite simply, another world. Icons provided windows into it; but Dionysius' frescoes seem almost to roll back the roof and lift us through broad northern skies into the heavenly world itself. Medallions of saints, the miracles of Jesus, the seven ecumenical church Councils, the outsized figures of angels and archangels, saints and evangelists—all seem to float in celestial blue and white.

Every vault and arch and pillar and wall is covered with figures in soft colors drawn from nature: the lavender and pink of northern flowers, the light green of unripe rye, the ochre of harvest time. Visual effects continuously change as the slanting sun proceeds on its appointed rounds. The eyes of a huge St. Nicholas seem to be looking at a worshiper wherever he stands. But always and everywhere Mary is the focus of attention with her dark red robe and tranquil gaze highlighting her unique status as the Queen of Heaven.

Dionysius' images are more animated than Rublev's a century earlier, but at the same time more weightless and abstract. Many figures have no feet or tiny pointed ones. They are no longer walking on earth. The three horses carrying the three wise men have a combined total of only six legs. They are not approaching the manger, but soaring directly up to heaven in a kind of celestial ballet (see illustration 9).

This picture of the Three Wise Men is one of 25 illustrations of the *akathistos* hymn cycle in praise of the Virgin Mary, which dominates the interior at Ferapontov—seeming to lift dematerialized painting into the realm of music, the most immaterial of all the arts.

This ethereal world of beauty seemed to be God's compensation for the sufferings of a burdensome earthly life. Fighting and fire, hunger and disease—all made death a constant presence on the Russian frontier. But the harsher the conditions, the more tender the Russian images of the Mother-Protector. She was—to cite the names given two favorite icons—their "joy in all sadness," the one "through whom all things rejoice."

Mary was the ultimate mother figure in the overwhelmingly masculine world of monastic complexes and military units that colonized the Russian interior. The akathistos hymns were originally written to honor the Virgin's protection of Constantinople from a barbarian siege in the early seventh century. The *Pokrov* or Feast of the Protection of the Virgin assumed even greater significance in the Russian North than in Byzantium. It was the last feast before winter—providing assurance of Mary's protection against natural elements no less than human enemies.

Dionysius had created Mary's world—a heaven beyond earth—at Ferapontov. It was his last work, his vision of a world transfigured, his foretaste of the larger life he was about to enter. His earthly life had been full of tribulation. He had entered monastic orders after his wife had died; and his two sons apparently followed him into the monastery and assisted him with the painting at Ferapontov.

Dionysius had essentially been exiled to this remote

spot by Tsar Ivan III at a time when Russia was rent with inner conflict. Many people expected the imminent end of the world, because the church calendar had run out in 1492. But the end of the world was not the end of everything for Dionysius. Beyond time itself, and even in a seemingly God-forsaken place, there was still another world: a mother's world.

Holy pictures provided not just otherworldly consolation for the cruelties of life; they also offered reassurance that the force of sacred history lay behind the advance of Muscovite power. Ivan III, the first Russian ruler to be called "the Great," married in 1472 the niece of the last Byzantine emperor, who brought with her to Moscow a new imperial aura: the seal of a two-headed eagle and the title of Caesar or Tsar to replace that of "Grand Prince."

A totally new Cathedral of the Assumption was built inside the Kremlin in the 1470s by an Italian Renaissance architect. Its open interior had a spaciousness unprecedented in Russian churches. Saints and soldiers, sacred and secular subjects became intertwined in the rich iconography of this church as it became the place of coronation for future Russian Tsars.

Dionysius created for this church a great icon that illustrates the life of Metropolitan Peter, the first church leader to take up permanent residence in Moscow. Its final panel shows the founder of the new royal line, Ivan I, riding off triumphantly with Metropolitan Peter—church and state in perfect harmony. Even the mountains mimic the motion of their horses.

A series of new, white-stoned churches capped with golden cupolas seemed to transform the Kremlin into a "New Jerusalem" and Moscow into a "Third Rome" (the second Rome of Constantinople having fallen to the Turks in 1453). The bell tower of Ivan the Great soon rose up above all the churches to dominate the Kremlin skyline. Like the tower atop the Mount of Olives in Jerusalem, to which Russian pilgrims later dragged a giant bell across the desert without the aid of wheels, the Kremlin bells were thought to be "trumpets of heaven" that would announce the Last Judgment to God's people.

The apocalyptical blending of sacred and secular authority reached a feverish climax in the reign of Ivan the Terrible, the grandson of Ivan III. He ascended to the throne at the age of three in 1533, was the first to be crowned Tsar in 1547, and stayed in power longer than any other head of state in Russian history (until 1584).

Ivan made Russia into an empire, but destroyed forever its inner peace. His troops swept down to the Caspian Sea, across the Urals into Siberia, and west to the Baltic. Along the way he destroyed Russia's main center of representative government, westward-looking Novgorod, killed the head of the Church and his own son and namesake, and established Russia's first version of a secret police: his new band of *Oprichniki*, armed men "set apart" for direct service to the Tsar.

None of this would have been possible if Ivan had not wrapped himself in the mantle of faith and disguised his hooded personal army as a kind of monastic order. His brutalizing conquests under the cloak of religion began when he built a massive missionary and military complex on the island of Sviiazhsk in the lower Volga. Logs were floated down the river to build a kremlin on Sviiazhsk even larger than that in Moscow. Within this new kremlin a new stone Cathedral of the Assumption was rapidly constructed. And within the sanctuary, the very "holy of holies" of the cathedral, the image of a living ruler of Russia was introduced into a holy painting for the first time in Russian history.

A full length picture of Ivan was placed alongside a fresco depicting "the great procession" of saints bringing bread and wine to the altar. This was only the beginning of Ivan's artistic deification, which became intense after his successful conquest of the great Tatar stronghold of Kazan 30 kilometers south of Sviiazhsk in 1553.

Ivan built the world-famous Kazan (or St. Basil's) Cathedral on Red Square in Moscow to memorialize the victory. Its reddish bricks capped with nine swirling towers suggested to some the flames of a giant candle burning in front of a Kremlin that was seen as the "living icon" of a New Jerusalem. The main entrance to the Kazan Cathedral, known as "the entrance into Jerusalem," was the starting point for the religious processions with political overtones that began to occur regularly through Red Square into the Kremlin. Subsequent Tsars tried to adorn the Kremlin with the 12 gates and other attributes of the final, celestial Jerusalem described in the Book of Revelation.

Russia's propensity for authoritarian cruelty with tinges of paranoia is often traced to Ivan. Yet ordinary Russians began to develop a certain nostalgia for the awesome Ivan once his troubled successor, Tsar Boris Godunov, was racked by famine, Polish invasion, and Russia's first great "Time of Troubles." Boris had become in 1598 the first Tsar to be chosen by a conciliar body rather than by inheritance; and Russia's suffering was popularly attributed to the untraditional basis of his authority, his interest in Western reforms, and his partly Tatar ancestry.

Boris had been the dominant power behind the throne of his sister's husband, Tsar Theodore, son of Ivan IV who succeeded him as Tsar in 1584. The only other lineal descendent of Ivan IV, the nine-year-old Prince Dmitry, was murdered in 1591, and the myth was born thereafter first that Boris had killed him and then that Dmitry had, nevertheless, somehow lived on as the rightful Tsar. The dynastic crisis became acute when Tsar Theodore died, and Boris was officially crowned successor. A false Dmitry was backed by the Poles, who conquered Moscow and crowned the pretender as Tsar in 1605. Starvation, rebellion from below, and court intrigues all ran amok until an army from the upper Volga region liberated Moscow and installed the new Romanov dynasty in 1613.

Though Tsarist authority was reestablished for 300 years under the new line, real power initially still lay with the monastic establishment. The power behind the new Tsar Mikhail was his father Filaret, the Patriarch of Moscow who himself used the imperial title "Great Sovereign" (*Veliky Gosudar*); and the first two-thirds of the 17th century were consumed by one last great effort of the Russian Orthodox Church to reestablish and extend its authority over all of Russian life.

Unlike Moscow, the Monastery of the Holy Trinity never fell to the Polish invaders. The new position of Patriarch of Moscow (established in 1589) emerged as the real locus of legitimacy for a Russia recovering from the chaos that followed the death of Boris Godunov.

Patriarch Hermogenes (1606–12), who had previously been the missionary Metropolitan of Kazan, became the hero-martyr of the "Time of Troubles." He starved himself to death in 1612 within the monastery inside the Moscow Kremlin where he had been imprisoned. He was protesting Russia's seeming apostasy to Catholicism—after sending the appeal to leaders from the interior of Russia that led to the expulsion of the Poles and installation of the Romanovs a year after his death. Hermogenes' successor, Patriarch Filaret, was the controlling force over the first Romanov Tsar Mikhail; and the greatest of all Russian church leaders, Patriarch Nikon, exercised equal power over the second Romanov Tsar Alexis during his stormy Patriarchate from 1652–67.

An ascetic, six-foot-six-inch monk from the trans-Volga region, Nikon tried systematically to introduce uniformity and discipline into Russia's resurgent but chaotic religious life. His reforms, however, split the church irrevocably—and paved the way for a new secular state to replace the old religious civilization of Muscovy and for a new service aristocracy to replace the monastic establishment as the cultural elite of Russia.

Western influences had continued to pour into Russia—and were popularly blamed for convulsions like the urban riots in 1648–50 and the black plague in 1653–54. Hostility was directed outward into violent actions on a massive scale never before seen in the Orthodox East: the massacre of Jews in Ukraine and Belorus in 1648 and the war launched in 1654 to recapture Orthodox Ukraine and Belorus from Catholic Poland.

As the Tsar was preoccupied with foreign war, Nikon assumed the title of Great Sovereign and attempted to set up a virtual domestic theocracy: correcting the printed editions of church books, the forms of worship, and the style of architecture. Ostensibly seeking Greek models (simple hemispheric domes and cruciform churches rather than onion domes and irregular shapes like St. Basil's), he relied more on the apocalyptical and prophetic Semitic branch of Orthodoxy (Syrian, Palestinian) than on more philosophical and scholarly Greek sources. He intensified the sense that in a time of such bewildering change and widespread suffering, history itself might be coming to an end.

Nikon was seen, in effect, as instituting simultaneous revolutions in both how authority is communicated (substituting printed books for oral tradition) and how authority is legitimized (substituting a centralized and tightened hierarchy for the more informal and decentralized authority of monks, holy men, and local parish priests). As the enormously expanded Russian army defeated Poland, recaptured Kiev, and brought much of Ukraine and Belorus under Russian rule, a more westernized clergy flooded into the Muscovite hierarchy.

Traditionalists believed that Nikon was seeking to replace the organic religious civilization of Muscovy with a papal theocracy. The traditionalists began to see Nikon as the Antichrist, drawing imagery from the apocalyptical, anti-Catholic writings that the Orthodox Ukrainians had used to defend their faith when under Catholic Poland. Many of the non-monastic "white" clergy joined the fiery Archpriest Avvakum in rejecting not merely all of Nikon's reforms, but all church innovations introduced since the time of Ivan the Terrible. The great monastic redoubt in Arctic Solovetsk refused to accept Nikon's new church books in 1657, and resisted a siege from 1668 to 1676 to become legendary hero-martyrs of the Old Belief along with Avvakum, who wrote the first autobiography in Russian history, before being burned alive in 1682. One of the greatest historical paintings of the 19th century shows the Boyaryna Morozova, the widow of Tsar Alexis' original tutor, making a defiant two-fingered sign of the cross (the Old Believer practice forbidden by Nikon) as she is born away to Siberian exile on a sled (see illustrations 10 and 11).

The traditionalists were officially condemned in the Church Council of 1667 as schismatics (*raskolniki*). But they were popularly admired for the intensity of their faith—which occasionally led them to burn themselves alive rather than to risk contamination with westernized ways. Old Believer communities lived simple, disciplined lives, working productively under austere conditions in the continuing expectation that the Last Judgment was imminent. They were persecuted by church and state alike, and, like those who were simultaneously fleeing west to America to escape religious persecution in western Europe, Russian Old Believers fled into the eastern interior of Russia, which now reached all the way to the Pacific.

Nikon himself had been banished from Moscow by Tsar Alexis long before Peter the Great formally abolished the Patriarchate in 1721. Nikon had created his own messianic redoubt, the Monastery of the New Jerusalem, in Istra just west of Moscow. After the Church Council of 1667, Nikon was exiled for life to Ferapontov with no consoling companionship except that of the heavenly host in Dionysius's frescoes. In the adjacent lake Nikon created one of the last and bleakest of all the "deserts" of frontier monasticism—building an artificial

THE FACE OF RUSSIA

island out of stones which he carried out into the lake one by one in order to create a secure place for uninterrupted prayer.

The great schism (*Raskol*) in the Russian church destroyed the authority of both the new ecclesiastical hierarchy and of the old grass-roots traditionalists. The net result was the permanent subordination of the Russian Orthodox Church to the secular state. Henceforth, Russia was to be a deeply divided country. The monastic culture of Muscovy was not destroyed; it was simply dispersed into the deep interior of the expanded Russian empire. At the same time, the agrarian peasantry was frozen into perpetual serfdom in 1648 by Russia's first law code (and first secular book ever printed in vernacular Russian), and the recurrent tradition of violent peasant rebellion tinged with religious prophecy began in 1667 with the great uprising of Stenka Razin. At its height in 1670 this uprising exercised power over most of the lower Don and lower Volga regions and commanded an army of 200,000 that killed off landowners and intensified the surviving aristocracy's sense of dependence on the central state for the maintenance of elementary order.

Nothing more dramatically illustrates the collapse of the old monastic culture during this turbulent period than the sudden and total transformation of Russian painting. Though the subject matter remained largely religious until well into the 18th century, the spirit was totally changed by the 1670s. Icons became lifelike and three-dimensional—in effect Western-type paintings with natural perspective and a miscellaneous clutter of decorative objects in the background. Tsar Alexis hired foreigners to paint the new icons in the armory of the Moscow Kremlin rather than relying on monks to paint them in monasteries. The most famous icon from this imperial workshop reduced the Vladimir Mother of God to the function of genealogically legitimizing the family tree of the Romanov dynasty (see illustration 12).

Eight centuries of pictorial Christian culture were, in effect, cast aside by Peter the Great and replaced by the new, purely secular court portraiture of his successors. Icons continued to be venerated, particularly in the provinces. But the authentic older icons gradually disappeared behind a layer of soot from the candles of worshippers. Ethereal frescoes were painted over with more naturalistic pictures. The old, otherworldly paintings were completely marginalized in the new aristocratic culture that radiated out from the new capital of St. Petersburg.

But different parts of this shattered art form returned from the cultural subconscious to help shape—for better or worse—modern Russian culture. Russians in the 20th century drew on the power of the icon tradition in three very different ways.

First of all, many Russians rediscovered icons as an aid to worship during the profound revival of Orthodox spirituality that began at the turn of the century. Since the time of Peter the Great, Russian culture had been basically dominated—as we shall see—by secular elites: a court aristocracy and then a critical intelligentsia. The Russian Orthodox Church had been literally as well as figuratively transformed into a subordinate ministry of state. Its head was a non-ecclesiastical "Over-Procurator" on the Swedish Lutheran model; and the Orthodox

Church played only a very minor role in the higher artistic and intellectual life of the late Romanov empire.

But Russia's creative "Silver Age" at the turn of the century was animated by a desire to rediscover the spiritual dimension of life amidst the growing materialism and vulgarity of modernity. The full beauty of the earliest and best icons was rediscovered through modern restoration methods; and a series of exhibitions caused many urbanized and hitherto secular Russian thinkers and artists to explore more deeply the faith that lay behind the art.

A Church Council in the Cathedral of Christ the Savior amidst the revolutionary unrest of 1917 re-created the Moscow Patriarchate; and despite the Bolshevik takeover, workshops for the restoration and study of icons continued to operate in the Monastery of the Holy Trinity and even inside the Moscow Kremlin during the first decade of Communist rule. A new generation of embattled believers rediscovered icons as "meditations in color" and aids to prayer.

As words were increasingly abused and distorted by demagogues preoccupied with short-term goals, pictures seemed to hold out the promise of reconnecting with older and perhaps more enduring truths. But both the old art and the old faith were systematically ravaged and nearly destroyed by the depredations of the "League of the Militant Godless" and other atheistic zealots that Stalin unleashed on Russia in the 1930s.

At the same time, however, Stalin and his henchmen were drawing on a second element of the icon tradition in order to destroy its primary, religious function. Stalin in a way coopted the propagandistic quasi-political function of icon painting even as he systematically razed churches and destroyed icons. Having received his only formal education in an Orthodox seminary, Stalin created for the masses a new orthodoxy without Christianity; and he used pictorial art to sanctify his own political authority.

Icons had been carried into battle, associated with victories, and even used to glorify other icons—as in the Novgorodian icon that shows an icon of the Virgin miraculously repelling a 12th century Suzdalian attack (see illustration 13). Holy pictures played a central role in dramatizing a procession and indicating precedence among leaders in Old Russia. Later Tsars seeking legitimacy sometimes included themselves in holy pictures or depicted themselves as iconographic figures. Ivan the Terrible may even have been responsible for having a procession of the Archangel Michael and the heavenly host from Sodom to the New Jerusalem depicted in a way that suggested his own triumphant return from sacking the Tatar "Sodom" of Kazan to the Russian "Jerusalem" of Moscow (see illustration 14).

The endless parades that Stalin staged through Red Square on the revolutionary feast days of May 1 and November 7, mimicked the religio-political processions that had previously been held there on Christian holidays. Stalin always stood at the center of a carefully arranged hierarchy of leaders atop the mausoleum that contained the mummified body of Lenin. It was eerily reminiscent of old Russia, where a carefully ordered hierarchy of holy figures on an icon screen was often raised over the buried body of a local saint. In place of Christ, the Savior at the center of every icon screen was now the new secular god Stalin, whom many believed to be the Antichrist. Sanctifying everything was the idolized corpse of Bolshevism's founding father, Vladimir Lenin, whose hands were folded out like those of the mummified bodies of Russian Orthodoxy's earlier founding fathers in the caves of Kiev.

A third legacy of the ancient icon tradition was its decisive impact on the birth of modern art. Restoration at the turn of the century of the full colors and graceful original lines of the best icons presented a new generation with a previously inaccessible artistic repertoire of semi-abstract patterns and deeply layered colors. Young artists were inspired by the icons' unique ability to convey austere purity in recognizable human form.

Kandinsky's abstract expressionism grew out of his own early immersion in the abstract and expressive religious art of Old Russia. Kandinsky took from icons their musical qualities, his belief in "the spiritual in art" and his fascination with white horses that seem to lead us into another, better world. Malevich took the geometric and cruciform shapes of his "suprematist" art out of the patterns of decorations on the robes of saints in the old icons. Lenin's Mausoleum in Red Square resembles the simple shapes of his early paintings; and Malevich's most famous late canvas, Red Cavalry, brings the richness of color of the restored icons to his secular reshaping of the old iconographic image of horses in holy procession (see illustration 15).

The rich colors of the restored icons reached across confessional lines to affect many gifted Jewish painters in the late imperial and early Soviet period—particularly Marc Chagall, whose prodigious flood of color has buoyed up both temples of faith and homes of music from Israel to France to America. Even modern paintings of the nude human body—a subject totally alien to the chaste and dematerialized world of old Russian painting—often show unexpected similarities to formal patterns used in icon painting. Vladimir Tatlin's semi-abstract woman has lines like those of a Deposition from the Cross (see illustration 16); Kuzma Petrov-Vodkin's boys, rhythmic motions like those of the disciples falling away from Christ in an icon of the Transfiguration (see illustration 17).

Many in post-Communist Russia today are attempting to resume the recovery and restoration of old icons and the reverential painting of new ones in the old manner. The medieval tradition of painting has probably been more fully revived in Russia than in any other major country in recent years. The process began—like so much else—amidst the confusions of the so-called cultural thaw under Nikita Khrushchev in the early 1960s.

Although Khrushchev had denounced some of Stalin's crimes in 1956 he had also sought to revive Communist ideology among the young by promoting radical causes in the Third World and a fresh wave of religious persecution at home. Under Khrushchev (1954–64), young people began seeking not just greater contact with the West, but also deeper knowledge about their own buried past. Icons began turning up everywhere as Khrushchev shut down churches and seminaries. The gathering-in of icons became a major summer activity for many. Popular interest continued to grow in this, the first great area of Russian artistic achievement, throughout the "time of stagnation" under Leonid Brezhnev (1964–82). Popular respect and reverence for icons has expanded rapidly ever since. But the destruction, dispersal, and neglect have been so great—and the human and financial resources for restoration are now so limited—that the full recovery of this heritage is still only a distant dream.

Enough has survived and been reassembled, however, to permit us to recognize that old Russian icon screens—like medieval stained glass windows and early modern ceiling paintings in Western churches—represent one of the great visualizations of the Christian faith. Unlike the other two, icon screens do not rest on illusion—neither the illusion that walls have become weightless as in a Gothic cathedral nor that the ceiling opens up to heaven itself as in a Baroque church.

Icon screens do suggest, however, more than those Western pictorial ensembles, that the divine world was rigidly hierarchical. The long practice of common worship before such an imposing image of unchangeable order may have subliminally helped legitimize the layering and sense of fixed place in society that limited individual freedom for so long inside Russia.

In perfecting a form and spreading a faith, Russian monks went through a process of artistic creation that was to be repeated time and again as Russia attained greatness and sought to solve its problems through other art media. In painting—as, later, in architecture, literature, music, and film—Russians first take over wholesale the finished version of a new art from an erstwhile enemy (painting from Byzantium). They then do something profoundly original with it (dematerialize its form and expand its function). They then so overload the art form with functions and messages and hopes for deliverance that the art medium essentially collapses of its own weight and loses its authority and evocative power in so-ciety. Only fragments of its former self are left behind, but they live on subconsciously to haunt—and occasionally to inspire—subsequent generations.

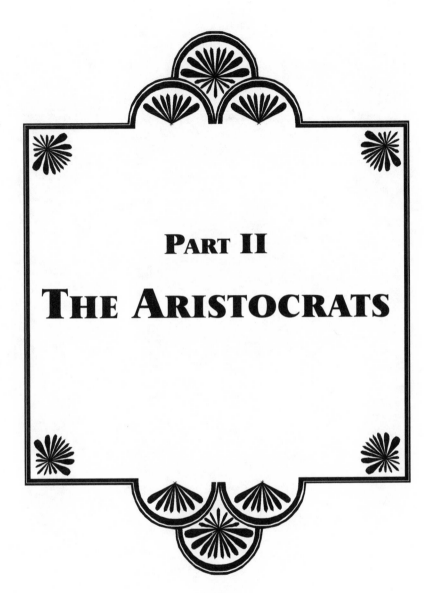

PART II

THE ARISTOCRATS

At the turn of the 18th century, Peter the Great became the first Russian ruler to visit western Europe. The sweeping modernizing reforms that followed created a new cultural elite, the Russian aristocracy, and a new capital city, St. Petersburg, as a "window to the West."

Peter stripped away—both literally and figuratively—the external features that had permitted the old, semi-independent hereditary lords, the boyars, to resemble monks: full-length beards and long black robes. The new aristocracy shaved and wore short, European-style coats (see illustration 11). They were now servitors of the State more than sons of the Church. They were collectively called *dvorianstvo* or "men of the court." They sought legitimacy in the cities and palaces of governance rather than in the monasteries and cathedrals of faith.

The new center of culture was radically different from the preceding capitals of Kiev, Vladimir, and Moscow. Each of these cities had obscure origins lost in the mists of time, and was located on a raised place far up a river in the deep interior of Eurasia. Each had expanded out slowly and organically in concentric circles from the relatively protected core.

In sharp contrast, Petersburg was a totally new city artificially thrust up almost overnight on flat and swampy terrain where no permanent settlement had ever existed before. It was built on the far periphery of the empire, shaped by straight rather than curved lines, and constructed at an immense cost of human life.

The new imperial city was baptized with the Dutch name of Sankt Peterburkh; but was subsequently known by many others: figuratively as the Palmyra, Venice, or Babylon of the north; popularly simply as Piter; officially in the 20th century alone as St. Petersburg, Petrograd, Leningrad, and now full circle back to St. Petersburg.

This was the city in which Russians reached their zenith of original accomplishment in two successive art media: architecture in the 18th century and literature in the 19th. In both cases Russians went through the same cycle they had experienced with painting: initial borrowing from a foreign model followed by innovations of stunning originality, but ending in a breakdown of the medium and a breakup of their own achievement.

Throughout this early modern or imperial period, Russian culture was created by aristocrats. Their influence radiated out from Petersburg and its surrounding palaces just as decisively as had medieval culture from Moscow and its neighboring monasteries. The high walls and white stone of the old capital were replaced by the broad boulevards and granite embankments of the new.

The monasteries of Old Russia had often doubled as fortresses, but they had always been open to all for pilgrimages and special feasts. The palaces of the new Russia were built during the long peace that followed the end of the Great Northern War with Sweden in 1721; but they were closed to anyone but fellow aristocrats. (Servants were confined to cramped quarters on the lower floor.) Old Russia had been mired in poverty and periodically ravaged by fire, famine and plague; but it was only in the new imperial Russia that class lines became all but impossible to cross.

The new aristocratic culture created—literally—a change in the face of Russia. The facelift was more than cosmetic when Peter cut away the facial hair and natural beards that had previously covered the faces of his entourage and artificially superimposed powdered wigs, waxed moustaches, and sculptured sideburns on their newly shaven surfaces.

The new aristocratic creators also used their hands differently. They no longer painted two-dimensional images of the heavenly world that God had revealed to all men through time. They now sculpted three-dimensional buildings and statues to legitimize their own worldly control over those of lesser rank in space. And some aristocratic hands eventually turned to writing in order to express both the suffering and aspiration of the human faces hidden behind the facades of power.

The Muscovite megalomania of Ivan the Terrible and his successors had created the appetite for a truly monumental city like imperial St. Petersburg—and, therefore, unintentionally helped destroy the very monastic culture they had sought to promote. In like manner, the new aristocrat culture of Petersburg created the verbal facility and spare time for the wandering imagination that unwittingly helped incubate a utopian revolution. That upheaval, in turn, ended up destroying the very aristocratic culture that had originally thought up the idea of a secular utopia.

Thus, in the broad sweep of history, Petersburg can be seen as the *mise-en-scène* for the most momentous development in modern Russian culture: its progression from religion to revolution. Whether this transformation is seen as an heroic epic or a terrible tragedy, it is a story worth lingering on for its own sake—not just because of its dramatic denouement in the 20th century, but because the 18th-century settings were so spectacular and the 19th-century scripts so moving.

The mass culture of 20th-century Russia has been haunted and inspired by the surviving fragments of its aristocratic no less than its monastic past. My own fascination with Russia did not grow out of any familial Slavic ancestry or links with either monastic or aristocratic culture. It originated in successive early encounters with Russian architecture and Russian literature.

I discovered at the age of ten in the Soviet building at the New York World's Fair of 1939 models of giant projects which this strange distant society was allegedly building and which in their pretentious enormity seemed unlike anything I had ever seen before. Three years later I read Tolstoy's *War and Peace* while the Battle of Stalingrad was raging and discovered a book that was longer and deeper than anything I had ever read before. I was directed to this marathon reading project by an émigré Russian woman who suggested that it might answer my question of why the Russians had been able to hold out against Hitler while others failed. I learned that better answers might be found in yesterday's book than in today's newspaper; and I began to learn about the vast suffering both that others had imposed on Russians and that they had inflicted on themselves.

The characters I kept meeting in Russian literature all seemed to be extensions of Pierre Bezukhov in *War and Peace*: wanderers in search of truth. Their armies had somehow defeated Napoleon and the most formidable army ever seen up to that time (as they were then doing with Hitler's). Yet, for Tolstoy, the simple, faceless people were really making history; and Tolstoy himself, having written the greatest epic novel of all time, basically renounced his craft for the last 35 years of his life, living in the countryside as a rustic, semi-peasant moralist.

How could a high aristocrat like Tolstoy, who had a loving family and knew well the glories of high culture in St. Petersburg, end up dying as a lonely wanderer and choose as his only gravestone a single green seedling in a small clearing within a forest? Moving from literature to history in search of answers, I discovered the group that Tolstoy himself had originally intended to write about in his novel: the idealistic aristocratic officers who had tried to bring constitutional reforms into autocratic Russia after the defeat of Napoleon. As these so-called Decembrists were being led away to execution or exile after a brief demonstration in Petersburg in 1825, a perplexed Tsarist official wrote that he could understand the French bourgeoisie making a revolution to gain rights. But how, he asked, is it possible to understand the Russian aristocracy making a revolution to lose them?

Architecture and literature—the two great forms of artistic expression perfected by the Russian aristocracy in the Romanov era—may provide clues to answering these difficult questions. Mastery of painting in new monasteries had helped faith conquer a frontier, and, by the end of the 17th century, Russia's borders extended to the Pacific. The building of new palaces in Petersburg during the 18th century helped aristocrats believe that a city could control the country. The invention of a new aristocratic literature in the early 19th century suggested that this—and perhaps the new capital of Petersburg itself—was an illusion.

Designed as a rival to Rome (and named not for Peter the Great, but for the Apostle Peter), its aristocratic, imperial architecture was indelibly shaped by a Russified Italian, Bartolomeo Rastrelli. But the subjugated country-side found its revenge through a new kind of prose litera-ture which a Russified Ukrainian, Nikolai Gogol, brought from the steppe to the city. He took Petersburg by storm and then left it to become the ultimate "wanderer over the Russian land"—making the *troika*, a carriage with three horses, as much a symbol of modern Russia as was Rastrelli's Winter Palace.

Gogol in his late years renounced his own artistic quest even more decisively than Tolstoy was to do. He burnt his last work, starved himself to death, and left behind what was to be the first in a long line of never-completed mega-lomanic trilogies by modern Russian artists. But, like Dostoevsky's *Brothers Karamazov*, Musorgsky's *Boris Go-dunov*, and Eisenstein's *Ivan the Terrible*, Gogol's *Dead Souls* was a towering masterpiece in itself. Rastrelli can be said to have completed a trilogy of his own: the three great imperial palaces in and around Petersburg: the Winter Palace on the Neva River, the inland Palace at Tsarskoe Selo, and the Summer Palace on the Baltic Sea at Peterhof.

Discovering and rediscovering such masterpieces in the course of visits to Russia over 40 years has served to rein-force the impression made on me by those giant architec-tural models of 1939 and by the giant novel I read during World War II—that this is a people who think big. Indeed, their unfinished works often seem larger in scope—and in some ways even more complete—than the polished final products of other great artists. But the broken lives of so many Russian creators make it clear that they themselves were rarely satisfied with what they had accomplished.

Real human anguish lay behind—and superhuman aspiration lay beyond—even their greatest achievements.

Returning in this section to my original sources of fascination with Russian culture, architecture and literature, I am impressed anew with how much modern Russian artists have been weighed down with what can perhaps be described as metaphysical overload. The new, purely secular arts of post-Petrine architecture and literature seem to have reflected—in some ways even to have magnified—the earlier monastic belief that art was designed for salvation rather than entertainment; and that artists should transform, and not merely ameliorate, the human condition.

Chapter 2

The Facade of Power: The Architecture of Rastrelli

The wooden architecture of Old Russia reached its greatest heights—both literally and figuratively—in churches and towers. From inside the protective walls of a monastery, kremlin, or fortress these silhouettes lifted up the gaze of ordinary Russians from the flatness of their daily lives. And if there were no fortified citadels where Russians lived and worked, they would often build a church in the shape of a tent-like tower—usually on a cleared high place where it could be seen from afar, carpeted by green in the summer and snow in the winter. In times of trouble, Russians sometimes assembled with axes at dawn in order to raise up a small church before sunset on the same day as an act of repentance and as a votive offering for God's protection.

To achieve a vertical thrust through horizontal log construction, hexagonal, rectangular, and (most often) octagonal shapes were piled atop each other. Where attainable, larch was used at the base, pine on top, and fir logs with strong roots to secure the roof. Shingles were cut by axe and sealed thereby (as sawed wood never could be) against the great enemy of moisture and rot.

Among the pagan Slavs on the exposed eastern frontier of Europe, the watchtower and alarm bell (striking a wooden board with a wooden mallet) came long before the bell tower and church bells of Christianity. Sheer survival depended on getting early warning of an impending attack. The oldest Slavic word for tower was *vezhi:* from *vedat,* to know. Knowledge was not theoretical in Old Russia; it was a practical matter of knowing whether they were about to be attacked by either of the two most dreaded forces on the wooded frontier: forest fire or foreign invaders. With the advent of gunpowder in the 14th century, Russians could rain down fields of fire on their human assailants; and the new word for towers became *strelnitsi:* from *streltsi,* shooters.

Watchtowers and bell towers were covered with roofs that increasingly acquired the shape of tents. In the Russian North, this was a practical necessity for shedding snow—as was the stretching out of the hemispheric dome into the characteristic onion dome atop the church itself. But these, the two original shapes of Old Russian architecture, also had powerful symbolic meaning.

The word for tent roof (*shatyor*) was taken from Persian and retained an aura of mystery and majesty. As Russians journeyed ever deeper into Eurasia, they associated the shape with the original holy space that God had created for the people of Israel on their way to the Promised Land: the tented tabernacle of Moses.

Movement in Muscovy was always a form of pilgrimage fraught with risk—of moral pollution in "unclean lands" on the way to working in a field; of devilish temptations on the way to worshipping in church; and of imperfect purification for a once-in-a-lifetime pilgrimage to Jerusalem or some great monastery. The tented tabernacles dotted across the countryside gave ordinary Russians reassurance that there were oases in the desert: sacred space even in remote places.

The word for onion dome (*lukavitsa*) suggests the vegetable itself. A popular Russian legend told of the Virgin Mary in her compassion lowering an onion down to pull a suffering sinner out of hell. As recounted in Dostoevsky's *Brothers Karamazov*, the sinner then fights off others who also grab on to the onion. It breaks and sends them all back into the flames.

Russians sought to avoid that fate by coming together on major feasts to worship in a cathedral topped at the center by a large onion dome. It was usually gilded, and glittered like the sun—reflecting rays of light downward through the forest even after the slanting northern sun seemed already to have set. Light was shining in the darkness—as it did when believers carried lighted candles out of church into the streets and countryside at Epiphany. This "feast of lights" tended to be more meaningful in the dark dead of a northern winter than Christmas itself. Ordinary people were carrying out into their own lives the "light of the world" that the wise men had first seen long ago in Bethlehem.

Carved images of the sun were everywhere in Old Russia. The sun was thought to go underground at night, but was symbolically greeted first at sunset and then at dawn by the little suns carved on the flat boards that covered the ends of logs under the gabled roofs at either end of a wooden dwelling. At noon, the sun shone on smaller flat boards carved with even bigger suns that hung straight down from the outside apex of both gables. These boards represented "the purity of human intentions, inextricably interwoven with the sunlit rapture of life itself and the victory of light over darkness." Their name (*polotentsa*) came to be used for any textiles (and eventually for the towels) that were hung inside. Carved horses suggesting the pagan sun god often curled off the end of a gable. Circular suns were often placed on the prows of boats (see illustration 18), the boards of spinning wheels, and the window frames (*nalichniki*) even of humble wooden houses.

The characteristic old Russian church was divided into three parts—each symbolically representing an aspect of Solomon's original temple in Jerusalem and a part of the Old Testament. There was the outer narthex (*trapeznaya*), the entry place for preliminary purification identified with the Book of Proverbs. Inside was the nave (*korabl*), where the congregation was enlightened spiritually as in the Book of Ecclesiastes.

Finally, at the east, was the sanctuary (*sviatilishche*) behind the icon screen. The term "altar" was generally used to describe this entire sacred space and not merely the holy table where the priest celebrated the mystic union between Christ and His Church suggested in the Song of Songs. So central was a church to the entire life of a community that a fourth part was often added beyond the narthex to the west: a "winged" entrance porch (*kryltso*) in which administrative and commercial matters could be conducted. All of this was generally built well above ground level in order both to rise over snowdrifts and to heighten the majesty of the church.

The walls and cathedrals of the Moscow Kremlin were permanently turned from wood into stone in the 15th century; and the wooden forms of tent roofs and onion domes were frozen into stone and brick in the towers of St. Basil's Cathedral in nearby Red Square in the 16th.

Alongside the rapidly proliferating body of new stone churches, there also emerged a new type of purely functional and rectangular stone building that was larger than any of the churches. Though generally still called a *trapeznaya*, these buildings either overwhelmed or were altogether detached from churches. They were, in effect, secular dining, reception, and residential halls designed more for civil authorities than for monks and pilgrims. The victory of this new type of building was assured by the simultaneous construction within the Monastery of St. Sergius and the Holy Trinity in the late 17th century both of a large trapeznaya and of a giant imperial residence (known once again by a noun derived from the Persian as the *tsarskie chertogi*).

Under Peter the Great, at the turn of the 18th century, an altogether new type of construction was introduced when he turned to redesigning the ravaged seaports of Azov and Taganrog that he had just captured from the Turks, on the Black Sea. The new architecture was called *regulyarnaya*, meaning both "regular" and "regulated." It sought to impose rigid rectilinear order on nature as well as on the irregularities of previous construction and of unplanned urban development. When he subsequently captured a foothold on the Baltic from the Swedes, he began to lay out plans for a new seaport that was to be even more severely "regular" on terrain that was far more irregular than anything ever tried before.

Peter's initial model was the canal-laced port of Amsterdam; and both the name he first gave the city and the style he initially imposed on it were Dutch. But Peter was at war for all but the last year of his 35-year rule, and he died before much was built that has survived. Floods replaced fire as the apocalyptical fear in Petersburg; and Peter died early in 1725 shortly before the first of the floods that seemed strangely to recur at hundred-year intervals, near the time of death of an innovative leader: Alexander I in 1825 and Lenin in 1924.

The new capital was Russia's first modern "crash project," forcibly imposed—like later Soviet ones—from the top down in order to "overtake and surpass the West." Peter's foe was Sweden, then the most advanced military power in Europe. But Peter followed the recurrent tendency of warring Russian leaders to take over the practices of a Western opponent. He reorganized the Russian government on the Swedish model with "colleges" rather than ministries for civil administration and a governmental "Over-Procurator" replacing a monastic Patriarch as the head of the Church.

In place of Moscow's chaotic, curvilinear streets and circular religious processions Petersburg built broad, straight boulevards or "prospects" suitable for military parades. And the new, Western-dressed regiments passed under triumphal arches replete with three-dimensional, often nude statues of mythological figures rather than the traditional ceremonial churches that stood over the entrance gate to a monastery and were adorned with icons of robed, two-dimensional saints. The embankments of the wide and threatening Neva River were lined with granite brought in from Finland, and Russians were for a time required to bring building stones with them when they came into the city.

Petersburg soon became a city of monumental architectural ensembles. Aristocrats from the provinces built palaces there in order to secure or improve their position on the new Table of Ranks, which awarded privileges on the basis of proven military or civilian service to the state. On the one hand, the aristocracy was opened up for entry and advancement according to criteria of merit rather than heredity. (Those of non-aristocratic origin who attained the fifth step became aristocrats for life; those who reached the ninth level could pass the title to their children.) But the net effect of this complex 14-level system was to swell the central bureaucracy that kept the records and to introduce even more rigid and hierarchical divisions into Russian society.

Much attention was devoted in the palaces of the upwardly mobile Petersburg aristocrats to designing the facade which everyone could see. The rectilinear building behind the facade enclosed the courtyard or *dvor*—providing, in effect, an aristocrat (*dvorianin*) with closed secular space for people of his social rank. Only rarely on special feasts would he venture forth into the open, sacred space of a church to worship in a conglomerate congregation as his predecessors might more frequently have done in the Muscovite past.

Eyes were lifted up in Petersburg not by tent roofs and onion domes, but by two Western-type spires atop the Admiralty building and the Cathedral in the Peter and Paul fortress, on either side of the Neva. The city seemed as relentlessly horizontal as the wide river that ran through it. And, as the number and size of its aristocratic buildings grew, they tended to blend together into a kind of continuous, intimidating facade. Tsars were now called emperors; and Petersburg seemed to be trying to enclose all Russian space into one giant imperial *dvor* for which Petersburg itself was the facade. As provincial centers imitated Petersburg, the imperial architecture of a city seemed to replace the icon screen in a church as the defining cultural symbol for the new Russia.

Yet Petersburg rapidly became something much more than a new center of power dominated by men in uniform and destined to become the crucible of revolution. It was transformed, in the half century after Peter the Great's death, into an open-air arena of dazzling beauty thanks largely to a remarkable architect, Rastrelli, about whose personal life—almost as much as in the case of Rublev—very little is known.

The culture of Muscovy had been exclusively masculine. The monasteries, fortresses, and frontier settlements of the Russian North—all were places where men lived without women and in virtual darkness for the long winter months. In contrast, the new aristocratic culture of Petersburg was essentially the creation of three women—Anna, Elizabeth, and Catherine—who ruled Russia for 66 years in almost uninterrupted succession from 1731 to 1796. They brought light into Russian buildings and enlightenment into Russian thinking. They turned Peter's still dark and wooden city into glittering gold—and at a latitude as far north as the middle of Hudson's Bay, where the sun was barely visible from late October through early March.

Consider the distance traveled from Russia's first large royal residence in the Moscow Kremlin under Ivan the Great to the ultimate imperial palace at Tsarskoe Selo outside Petersburg under Catherine the Great.

Women could not attend receptions in the late 15th-century Palace of Facets (*Granovitaya Palata*). They appear to have looked on only from a small viewing place cut out of the far wall just under the ceiling. In the nearby Terem Palace, where the Tsar formally resided, the Tsarina could enter only by a single, side door, and had access only to the small chapel and bedroom. The interior space was dark and cramped, and the exterior was jammed against a crowded jumble of churches and armories. Black-robed boyars could approach the Tsar's small and claustrophobic receiving room only through two even smaller rooms.

Ordinary Russians could only hope that someday their pitiful entreaties to their "little father Tsar," *Tsar-Batiushka*, might be placed in the basket that was occasionally hoisted up three stories to the distant "petition window." The words for this, the unique point of entry into the Tsar's court, *chelobitnoe okno*, literally meant "a window for beating one's head against the ground." This suggested both the prostration before God that believers made in church and the version of the oriental kow-tow that earlier Grand Dukes of Muscovy had themselves endured during their long years as collector of the annual Russian tribute to the Mongols.

In total contrast, by the mid-18th century, the royal receiving room at Tsarskoe Selo was a sea of light. Huge windows and mirrors lined two parallel enfilades more than 325 meters long, passing through glittering rooms that led to a dazzling, amber-lined waiting room and a throne room nearly 50 meters long at the very end.

On the throne sat not a Tsar weighed down with 80 pounds of dark robes, but an Empress in a white gown.

Out the windows on either side, a visitor would see not the walls of another building within a cramped kremlin, but magnificent vistas suggesting the extended power of an enlightened despot. On one side was the "parade courtyard" where carriages entered an enclosed semi-circular space and drove half-way up and all the way back to the far end of the long palace in a kind of preliminary pass-in-review before entering the near side of the palace for a long march back to the throne room (see illustration 19). Out the windows on the other side lay a landscaped park that reached into the only partly cleared countryside beyond. The palace itself seemed to be extending its power over nature by stages.

Visitors saw Russia emerging from darkness into light—rather in the way that the long dark alleyways of vaulted linden trees in the park at Tsarskoe Selo suddenly opened up onto cleared spaces bathed in sunlight that reflected off nearby streams and ponds. Even the closed and darkened alleyways of trees had an enlightened purpose: to shelter small birds from hawks. The pavilions within the clearings—like the great palace itself—brought the swirling decorations of the European rococo out of interior space onto the sculptured and rusticated exterior facades of buildings. It all seemed to illustrate the subject of the monumental fresco that covered the ceiling of the palace's throne room: Russia Enjoying the Bounties of Civilization.

The Germanophile Empress Anna first hired as chief architect of the imperial court Bartolomeo Rastrelli, who built Tsarskoe Selo. The Francophile Empress Catherine the Great first lived in it, causing it to be known popularly as Catherine's Palace. But it was the Italianophile

Empress Elizabeth who reigned between the two (1741–61) who conceived of this palace and gave free reign to Rastrelli to make St. Petersburg into the imperial city that still inspires awe today.

Elizabeth made the palace rather than the church the locus of legitimacy in Russia; the aristocratic court rather than the monastic compound the source of ritual and rhetoric for broader society. She turned Russia's westward gaze from the Germanic north that had fascinated Peter the Great's immediate successors to the Latin south, from the Baltic to the Mediterranean. She founded Russia's first university (in Moscow in 1755) and Academy of Arts (in Petersburg in 1757). She turned the face of Russia away from Christian icons in candlelit churches toward mythological statues in open gardens.

Elizabeth let the Russified Italian Rastrelli begin to transform the city that her father had founded into a kind of open-air theatrical setting for the aristocracy. There the masses would eventually enact the real-life drama of a two-act revolution in 1917. By then, the imperial family had long since retreated to the palace that Elizabeth had created but never lived in at Tsarskoe Selo. It deserved, far more than Rastrelli's more famous Winter Palace, to be renamed The Hermitage; because it was far away from the city and close to nature. The pavilions that dot its parks even today deserve the name "constellation" that Russia's first great scientist and polymath Mikhail Lomonosov bestowed on Tsarskoe Selo in his poetic tribute to the palace:

> ...Rome is being built in Russia
> The example is this home so glorious.

Now all who see it seem to say
That Rome will soon be shamed before us.

Elizabeth's collaboration with Rastrelli was in a way part of the posthumous legacy of her father, Peter the Great. He had summoned the architect's father, the sculptor and metal-worker Bartolomeo Carlo Rastrelli, to come to Russia in 1716 after the death of Louis XIV. The older Rastrelli had been working on the great palace of the Sun King at Versailles. His 16-year-old son was to build equally extravagant palaces for Peter's daughter Elizabeth, who seemed to spend her entire life inside one and planning the next.

Elizabeth was born in the last great wooden palace of Moscow at Kolomenskoe and died in the last great wooden palace in Petersburg, a temporary one built for her on Nevsky Prospect while the Winter Palace was being reconstructed in stone for the first time. But she left behind the three greatest stone palaces in Russian history—all built by Rastrelli—the Winter Palace at the heart of Petersburg and the two palaces just outside at Peterhof and Tsarskoe Selo.

Not just the name of the architect but the substance of his vision was Italian, and the model city was Rome. But it was a composite image of the imperial city of classical antiquity and the Palladian palaces of the Renaissance. The "third Rome" of Moscow seemed to be ceding pride of place to the "new Rome" of Petersburg. A secular Peter was the new rock on whom the empire had been founded, and he had been crowned with the Latin title of Imperator rather than the Slavic Tsar. Summoned by the new Peter to help cast cannon for the war with Sweden, the older Rastrelli cast the first equestrian statue of Peter the Great and Russia's first publicly displayed series of statues on a non-Christian, mythological theme. He scattered bronze figures from Aesop's fables along the left bank of the Neva, where his son Bartolomeo was eventually to raise up the mighty Winter Palace for the Empresses who succeeded Russia's first Emperor.

Bartolomeo Rastrelli built for the Empress Anna (1731–41) two residences in Moscow and both a summer and winter palace in Petersburg—all in wood. His transformation of Petersburg from a bleak Dutch naval base into a glittering baroque city began with the coronation of the Empress Elizabeth in Moscow in 1742 and her triumphal return to Petersburg in solemn procession. She was surrounded by an ornate profusion of temporary architectural facades, triumphal arches, and firework illuminations. As she settled in to the new capital, she gave Rastrelli, in effect, *carte blanche* to turn Petersburg into a city of permanent decorative facades and perpetual parades.

The imperial style that Elizabeth's architect imposed on Petersburg was, in the first instance, a celebration of Russia's newfound proximity to—and power over—the sea. Already in his wooden Winter Palace by the Neva in 1735, Rastrelli had raised up a glittering building with more than 200 rooms including a magnificent amber room where an unprecedented combination of windows, mirrors and amber spread light over the waters that only a decade before had flooded the city. Now, for Elizabeth, he built a new wooden summer palace with more than 160 rooms at the intersection of the two major canals of the city: the Fontanka and the Moika. Concurrently, he built yet another imperial residence, the Anichkov

Palace, at the intersection of the Fontanka canal with the main boulevard of the city: the Nevsky Prospect. This palace made its central courtyard into a lake accessible to boats from the canal—suggesting to many that the New Rome might also be a New Venice.

Statues of Neptune proliferated in the new capital; and mastery over the sea became the theme of the first of Rastrelli's three great royal palaces: Peterhof on the Gulf of Finland just west of Petersburg. Here Rastrelli first applied his distinctive talent for extending an existing palace to an extraordinary length—creating in effect a facade of power and the facing for a parade. And the palace faced the sea through a terrace of fountains that descended from its high perch to the gulf below (see illustration 20). The waters swirled at the behest of the sovereign around the central statue of Samson, the symbol of strength whose name was the Hebrew word for sun. The play of sunlight on the brightly colored stucco facade and cascade of fountains suggested in the brief northern summer of the midnight sun that it might even be possible to recreate classical Rome in the frozen north.

Rastrelli built smaller, but similar palaces in Petersburg for Elizabeth's leading aristocratic courtiers. Fountains cascaded down to the Fontanka Canal for the Vorontsov family, and at the intersection of the Moika Canal with the Nevsky Prospect for the Stroganovs. Imperial power seemed to be watching over all the strategic points on the city's waterways. So it seems appropriate that Rastrelli built the greatest of all his palaces—the Winter Palace we still see today—on the Neva River overlooking the place where it flows out into the Gulf of Finland, and on to the Baltic Sea and the Atlantic Ocean beyond.

This was the fourth such palace built on the same spot in Petersburg, but the tallest, largest, and first to be built out of stone. It towered over the nearby Admiralty Building of those days and dominated the Petersburg skyline. Its columns, pilasters, and bas reliefs spilled all the decorative techniques of interior architecture out into exterior decor. The palace faced the Neva on one side and huge open squares on the other three. In every direction it projected a colorful, but intimidating, facade of power. The 180 stone statues of classical gods and goddesses high up on the exposed roof-top seemed to defy nature itself with their tranquil nudity.

Rastrelli was creating a distinctive Russian architecture in order to validate imperial power. It differed from either the baroque or rococo in the West both by its distinctive, decorative use of the shapes of Russian church architecture and by its megalomanic attempt to project power into and over space. In effect, Rastrelli sought to suggest that imperial power could both coopt history and conquer nature. In many ways the hubris of modern Russia begins with his architecture—which soon gave rise to the thought that the new imperial city might be, after all, a new Babylon rather than a new Rome.

Rastrelli placed a huge sculpture of a two-headed eagle, the imperial insignia, over the cupola at one end of Peterhof; and, at the other end, a small cruciform church with five onion domes. These characteristically Muscovite bulbs no longer enclosed holy space for worshipers inside a church at the center of a kremlin. They now provided a sculptured silhouette for promenaders to admire while passing by a decorative end piece on the far side of a lengthy palace.

In his new Winter Palace, Rastrelli marginalized the church as he had at Peterhof. It was only one of the three functional rooms off the main staircase in the middle. The other two were the small theatre and the throne room, itself a kind of theatre. The so-called "parade" or "Jordan" staircase led up majestically from the Neva (the new "Jordan River") through a string of "parade rooms" with a view of the Neva into the great throne room. The parquet floor used the cruciform image of five circles taken from Russian church architecture as a decorative motif. But in the center of the overall, square building it-self was simply a vast open space. It was the ultimate courtyard, the *dvor* that the *dvorianstvo* all wanted to pen-etrate—and at the same time, it symbolized the expanded space of an expanding Russia that imperial Petersburg was seeking to control.

The Winter Palace acquired an even more intimidat-ing elongation as it added and then absorbed an adjacent "Hermitage" (the present name for the entire complex) which in turn later blended into other adjoining struc-tures stretching out along the Neva into a seemingly un-ending monolithic facade. In the vast square on the op-posite side, imperial Russia mounted its largest and longest military parades.

The palace that most fully embodied the imperial at-tempt to mount parades and control space was Rastrelli's last and largest palace at Tsarskoe Selo. As with Peterhof and the Winter Palace, a preexistent building was elon-gated. But at Tsarskoe Selo an entire story was added; an unusually decorative five-domed church was raised up over the end point; and the gilding and coloring was the brightest of all his palaces.

Rastrelli also created three works of sculptured church architecture that were strikingly original. Each in its own way also projected imperial power out further—and up higher—than ever before.

In Kiev, he created perhaps the most beautiful baroque church in all the Russian empire in the wake of Elizabeth's triumphal visit to the "mother of Russian cities." This five-domed Church of St. Andrew was raised up atop a three-story pedestal on the side of the hill overlooking the Dnieper River where Prince Vladimir had allegedly brought Christianity to the Eastern Slavs. The church was named for the Apostle Andrew, who according to Slavic legend had come to Kiev even in biblical times just as Peter had gone to Rome. The four outlying domes are raised up on free-standing Corinthian columns rather than on drums, and the large central dome provides vertical uplift even in today's bustling Ukrainian capital.

Rastrelli sought to leave his stamp on Moscow as well—and continued his thrust upward by giving a baroque twist to the old Russian form of the tent roof. A century earlier, the authoritarian Patriarch Nikon had tried to regularize and control church architecture by outlawing tent roofs; and he had created a small model of the Church of the Holy Sepulchre in Jerusalem inside the main church of his own Monastery of the New Jerusalem at Istra just outside Moscow. Rastrelli tried to complete this project, and ended up embellishing and stretching out the central dome, punctuated with many windows, into an unusually broad tent roof.

This idea of asserting and augmenting authority by creating a vast central dome that will dominate all other buildings was realized a century later in a more classical style by two other foreign architects: Constantine Ton who built the Church of Christ the Savior which dominated the Moscow skyline, and Auguste Montferrand who designed the equally dominant St. Isaac's Cathedral in Petersburg.

Elizabeth's passion and Rastrelli's talent were perfectly fused in the Smolny Convent, the greatest creation of the distinctive Russian architectural style perfected by Rastrelli. It is usually characterized as imperial baroque, but would perhaps better be described as monumental rococo.

Superficially at least, Smolny was conceived as a traditional religious convent. It was given the name Resurrection-New Maiden along with protective, exterior walls and a central cathedral that Elizabeth had specified to be modeled on the Cathedral of the Assumption in the Moscow Kremlin. But Rastrelli made the central, five-domed church so compact and vertical that it seemed to have only one dome with a few rococo flourishes attached. Far more noticeable were the four single domes over the four corners of the outer walls. And those walls were used not for protection, but for the living quarters of the young noble ladies who were to be educated there.

Elizabeth made an enlightened school for women rather than a dark monastery for men the crowning ensemble in her city of light. Smolny was not just another facade of power and backdrop for military parades. It was the feminine face of Russia: a finishing school with a rococo tiara.

Elizabeth's palaces had turned wood into stone; her convent now turned tar (the literal meaning of *smolny*)

into gold. In the process, she turned aristocratic living inside out. She not only feminized the face of the convent, spreading interior decorative motifs all over its exterior facings. On the very spot where her father, Peter the Great, had processed tar for a brutalized navy, Elizabeth created a playful confection for a feminized aristocracy. Even today a visitor can not help but experience some measure of refining delight in contemplating Smolny's swirling ensemble of blue stucco and white decor capped by a five-domed polyphony of gold.

But Smolny was—like imperial Petersburg itself—a monument to aristocratic exclusiveness, and its architecture an embodiment of the imperial illusion of controlling space. The five largest domes of Rastrelli's great ensemble, in effect, enclosed outdoor space for promenades rather than an indoor place of worship. The central cathedral appeared to be one soaring, single central dome; the large, outlying bulbs on the four corners of the walls seemed from afar to represent the other four domes of a very wide and overextended version of a traditional pentacupolar and cruciform church.

Rastrelli had sought to expand the reach of Smolny up to the heavens as well as out to the countryside. He built an elaborate model for a bell tower designed to stand in front of the Cathedral at twice the height of the Bell Tower of Ivan the Great in the Moscow Kremlin. It was never built, but Rastrelli left behind a legacy of unfettered extravagance and artistic megalomania. Subsequent artists were infected by the dream that they too might create something equally grand and glorious—perhaps in some other medium, in some other way, or in some other place.

Elizabeth died in 1761 in the temporary wooden palace

on the Nevsky Prospect that Rastrelli had built for her while awaiting the completion of Tsarskoe Selo and the Winter Palace. Her successor, after the usual brief and turbulent interregnum, was Catherine the Great (1762–96). She was the last woman to rule Russia; and she proceeded to overlay Petersburg with even more great architectural ensembles. Her new style was more simple and classical, but the scale was equally monumental—and her attempts to conquer and control space even more ambitious.

Catherine systematically superimposed the artificial geometric grid patterns of Petersburg on provincial cities, confiscated monastic property, and dreamt of replicating Greek as well as Roman glory on Russian soil. After freeing Crimea from the Tatars, she gave a Greek name, Sevastopol (meaning both "august" and "imperial city"), to the new naval base she built on the site of an old Greek settlement, and considered renaming Tsarskoe Selo Constantingrad. She named the greatest of her monumental new classical palaces in Petersburg Taurida, the Greek name for Crimea; and the lover for whom she built it, Gregory Potemkin, "the Prince of Tauris."

He is, of course, best known as the alleged architect of "Potemkin villages," the portable facades that were designed to hide the misery of the people from her eyes during triumphal tours throughout the Empire. Facades were now protecting rather than projecting power; and a better-educated aristocracy was beginning to discover the human suffering that lay behind the facings on the palaces. They began to think about it, talk about it, and eventually write about it. The passion for great accomplishment was moving from architecture to books.

French became the language of aristocratic discourse

after Russia allied itself with France in 1756; and Catherine promoted the values of the French Enlightenment by corresponding extensively and publicly with the lions of the French Enlightenment, Voltaire and Diderot. She made the former the official historian of the Russian empire and bought the library of the latter. And she ordered from the French sculptor Etienne Falconet the bronze statue that was to become the symbol of imperial Petersburg, showing Peter the Great mounted on a rearing horse. It was placed in 1782 in the open Senate Square on the other side of the Admiralty from the Winter Palace.

The monumental Empire Style was added to Petersburg architecture during the reign of Tsar Alexander I (1801–25). The spire of the Admiralty was raised up even higher; and the entrance to the great Palace Square before the Winter Palace was adorned with the greatest of all Russian triumphal arches. Hopes for reform were raised when Russia defeated Napoleon—but were dashed when the aristocratic Decembrist movement was repressed in 1825 after an abortive demonstration in Senate Square. The failed uprising in the sight of the statue and a subsequent flood in Petersburg gave birth to one of the greatest of all Russian poems, *The Bronze Horseman*. Its author was Alexander Pushkin, who almost overnight and single-handedly made literature the dominant new art form of the early 19th century—and the new arena in which to pursue Russia's restless search for greatness.

Educated in the lycée at Tsarskoe Selo, Pushkin considered its gardens his home; and he made the heroic statue of Peter, the symbol of Russian power, rise up amidst the flood and pursue a beaten-down clerk. The suffering little man in the big city become one of the stock characters in Russia's belated explosion of a humanistic literature. Pushkin's poem soon attracted more attention than Falconet's statue. Pushkin more than any other person invented both the vernacular language and the distinctive literary forms of modern Russia.

Pushkin was a high aristocrat who, between two periods of public service in Petersburg, wrote a romantic poem on a folkloristic Russian theme (*Ruslan and Lyudmila* in 1820), narrative poems on exotic themes while in exile in the south (*The Prisoner of the Caucasus* in 1822, *The Fountain of Bakhchisaray* in 1824, and *The Gypsies* in 1827), then brought Shakespearean-type objectivity and grandeur to troubled episodes of Russian history through his epic poem *Poltava* of 1828, his dramatic tragedy of 1831, *Boris Godunov*, and his historical novel of the Pugachev rebellion against Catherine the Great, *The Captain's Daughter* in 1836.

Perhaps Pushkin's two most beloved and influential works were written in forms different from all of those mentioned above. His "novel in verse" *Eugene Onegin* provided a panoramic portrayal of provincial aristocratic life and created in the figure of Onegin, the original "superfluous man" of Russian literature. He and the idealized Tatyana were, in the words of the literary historian D.S. Mirsky, "the authentic Adam and Eve of the Mankind that inhabits Russian fiction." And, in the category of prose fiction, Pushkin produced an unforgettable short story, *The Queen of Spades*, which anticipated the psychological depth and fascination with gambling of Dostoevsky.

Pushkin died at age 37 in a senseless duel—as did the other great romantic poet of the era, Mikhail Lermontov, four years later at age 27. These tragedies ended prematurely the Golden Age of Russian poetry. But Russians of all persuasions ever since have generally placed Pushkin on an unreachable pedestal—and given poetry a special status in Russian culture. The musicality of Pushkin's verse was to inspire many of the greatest Russian operas. His passionate love of freedom and ability to empathize with all his variegated literary creations made Pushkin a belated conveyer of the kind of renaissance humanism that Russia had missed during its long cultural isolation.

Pushkin, in his great poem *The Prophet*, seems to have foreseen the more anguished type of art that was to become endemic in Russia after his death—and would deeply influence subsequent Russian history. Writing in 1826 at a time of sadness over the repression of the Decembrists, Pushkin describes how an angel of the Lord placed a living coal in the place where his "trembling heart" had been and bade him speak prophetic words that would burn "the hearts of people." This was the task essentially taken on by Pushkin's chosen successor as the literary leader of Russia: Nicholas Gogol. Through him, we can see an essential new art medium for Russia—prose fiction—go through the same cycle of first imitating foreign models, then doing something completely original, and finally being broken up altogether.

Chapter 3

Speech after Silence: The Literature of Gogol

Authoritarian rule was confirmed in Russia—seemingly forever—by the ascent to the throne in 1825 of the Prussophile Tsar Nicholas I. He wiped out the Decembrists, the last gasp of the aristocratic reform impulse that his Francophile predecessors had indulged at times. He crushed the Polish echo of the French Revolution of 1830 and absorbed what was left of an independent Poland into the Russian empire. And he formally proclaimed in 1833 that his empire was radically different from those of the West and based squarely on an ideology of Orthodoxy, Autocracy, and Nationality.

The "Official Nationalism" of Nicholas and his German wife was protected by censorship and by a new form of Secret Police (the so-called Third Section). It was celebrated by a seemingly endless series of parades in Petersburg. It was said that the Emperor viewed them as rehearsals for the Last Judgment, which would take the form of a final pass-in-review before God himself.

The Tsar was accountable to no one on earth. He was, literally, self-empowered (the meaning of autocrat, the Russian *samoderzhets*). His awesome authority seemed to be frozen into permanence by the neo-classical stone ensembles that his local governors and highest ranking aristocrats began to build in every important provincial center of the Empire.

Power was projected in every direction. The imperial parade had marched west to the Baltic, absorbing Estonia, Latvia, Lithuania, and Finland. A giant imperial square surrounded by neo-classical buildings was thrust into the heart of Helsinki, the new capital that Russia prescribed for Finland—bringing the capital nearer to Petersburg and replacing Abo (Turku) that had been close to Sweden.

The parade had gone south as well—down the picturesque Georgian Military Highway to absorb the ancient cultures of Georgia and Armenia, creating a new imperial city at the Russian end of this artery into the Caucasus bearing the appropriately imperial name of Vladikavkaz (literally "Rule the Caucasus"). And the parade continued far to the east. Scouts had moved down from Russian Alaska to establish an outpost at Fort Ross (from *Rossiia*, Russia) just north of San Francisco. And Russians were also to move down the Asian side of the Pacific, creating shortly after Nicholas' death Vladivostok (literally "Rule the East") at the mouth of the Amur River on the Chinese border.

In a way, it was all an extension of one of the greatest real-life military processions of all time: the triumphant Russian pursuit of Napoleon's Grande Armée across Europe in 1813–14. Russia had liberated Europe from the revolutionary dictatorship of Napoleon and the subversive arrogance of the Western Enlightenment. The enormous Russian army that entered Paris during Holy Week of 1814 had celebrated an Orthodox Easter liturgy en masse in the great open space where King Louis XVI had been guillotined. Its name had been changed from Place Louis XV to Place de la Révolution, but was henceforth to be Place de la Concorde. And the eternal concord among nations that was to prevail now and forever was assured not simply by a treaty among states, but by a "Holy Alliance" between the Three Kings (the Emperors of Russia, Prussia, and Austria) who had come from the East—like the Christmas wise men of old—to witness the birth of a new era.

This myth was shaken in the West by the revolutions of 1830, but was strongly reinforced in the East by Nicholas I. When a revolution for Polish independence swept over Poland late in 1830, Nicholas sent the Russian army in to reconquer the country. It amounted to a full-scale war followed by a Draconian peace of internal repression and forced Russification. When the West was convulsed by yet another contagion of revolutions in 1848–49, Russian military might once again intervened to crush the new independence of Hungary. The central metaphor of Nicholas's "Official Nationalism" was of Russia as the rock against which the waves of disruptive, revolutionary thought were beating in vain.

Russians held firmly to this image in part because of unrequited love. The Russian aristocracy had given its heart to France. They had established a cultural identity different from the Russian-speaking peasants and from the polyglot trading and professional class (who tended to speak German, Swedish, Yiddish, or Armenian) by speaking French among themselves. French Enlightenment ideas became fashionable during the reigns of Catherine the Great, who corresponded with Voltaire, bought Diderot's library, and drew up a never implemented program for political reform based on the works of Montesquieu. Even after the regicidal excesses of the French Revolution, Alexander I played with French ideas for reform implanted by his Franco-Swiss tutor and met with Napoleon on a raft at Tilsit in 1807 to forge an alliance that was to divide the world between these two powers.

Russia, therefore, considered itself betrayed as well as violated when Napoleon invaded Russia in 1812 with the largest army ever deployed up to that time. The aristocracy derided him as the "crowned Jacobin"; the peasantry wondered if he were the Antichrist.

Russia somehow survived and repelled the assault of the all-conquering Napoleon. It seemed truly miraculous and gave rise to supernatural explanations. The mysterious fires that leveled Moscow at the time of Napoleon's brief occupation seemed to have apocalyptical meaning. Muscovites were thought to be confronting Napoleon the way the Old Believers had faced Peter the Great—purifying themselves with fire rather than dissolving into Western corruption. The idea grew that Orthodox tradition and Russian togetherness (the Russian *sobornost*) had prevailed against Catholic cunning. Russia would somehow save Europe from itself—perhaps produce a "spiritual conquest of Europe" that would be even more glorious than the military conquest they had made by sweeping on to Paris in 1814.

The first step was to celebrate the salvation of Moscow and begin its resurrection. Already in 1812 Alexander I had commanded that a great memorial be built to "speak in stone" to all ages and all people about the victory.

Thus began an incredible search for a memorial that lasted till 1889. Russians believed that Christ had saved Russia, but they no longer thought of him as the simple, human savior that Rublev had depicted on his icon. Christ had to be embodied in a great work of architecture. Thus began the protracted, highly visible project that helped create the 19th-century Russian passion for sweepingly ambitious artistic projects, and eventually produced the largest church in Russian history: the Church of Christ the Savior.

A mystical Swedish painter and convert to Orthodoxy, Alexander Vitberg, initially came up with a gigantic proposal that would have turned the core of Sparrow Hills overlooking Moscow into a huge, classical shrine reaching from the river to the skies. He later modified this plan into a three-story giant church with innumerable classical columns. On the lower, underground level was a triangular base symbolizing the body; at ground level, a cruciform church representing the soul; above ground was an enormous hemispheric dome suggesting the spirit.

This was, in a way, the first of the great redemptive trilogies that artists in the 19th century would repeatedly attempt to realize but never complete. Vitberg was soon exiled; and Tsar Nicholas brought another Swede from Rome, Constantine Ton, to produce another design on another spot where a monastery had been at a picturesque bend on the Moscow River on the other side of the Kremlin from St. Basil's. Ton began in 1839 to build a five-domed, neo-Byzantine memorial that combined the functions of a war museum with those of a church. It was not finished until 1880, the year before Ton's death, and was not dedicated until 1889.

Ton transformed the skyline of central Moscow. The Church of Christ the Savior was higher than the Bell Tower of Ivan the Great. And the Kremlin itself was transformed into a massive ensemble by a great new palace complex with more than 700 rooms that Ton built there in the late 1830s and 1840s. The interior space in St. George's Hall, the Emperor's new reception area, was three times as large as that of its once dominant predecessor, the Palace of Facets.

Architecture under the active direction of Nicholas I was enclosing ever more space and reaching ever greater heights. Nowhere was this more dramatically demonstrated than in the reshaping of the vast Palace Square in front of the Winter Palace in Petersburg. It had long ago replaced Red Square in Moscow as the preferred location for a military review. The great square was newly enclosed across from the Winter Palace by the imposing semicircular General Staff Building centered on the most monumental of St. Petersburg's triumphal arches.

This was the square in which the great imperial parade began and ended. Alexander I had led the troops out from here to begin the long pursuit of Napoleon across Europe. The architect-engineer Auguste Montferrand had given the Tsar an album containing the sketch for such a memorial in Paris in 1814, and, 20 years later, Montferrand raised up the largest monolithic granite column in the world in the middle of the square in memory of the victorious Alexander.

Montferrand also brought to fulfillment in 1853 his 35-year project to build St. Isaac's Cathedral, the largest church with the largest undivided interior space in all Petersburg—as well as another imposing square behind it centered on an equestrian statue of Nicholas I. Everywhere one looked in the imperial city in the time of Nicholas, there were new architectural ensembles. The styles were more eclectic, but seemed to blend in to create the effect of an uninterrupted facade for a city of continuous parades.

Petersburg was no longer just a city of grey stone and pastel-colored stucco. St. Isaac's was adorned with malachite and marble, and its dome was so huge that it required elaborate cast iron support inside. (This revolutionary new form of construction was to become the model for the enlargement of the dome of the main building in another artificially created governmental city: the Capitol Building of Washington, D.C.) By the end of Nicholas' reign iron bridges had connected the mainland city with the islands across the Neva, and iron rail lines had linked Petersburg with Moscow.

The idea that Russia was the rock holding out against the waves of Western decadence seemed to be embodied in the stone and iron architecture of Imperial Petersburg. This nationalistic myth was woven into the architecture of the mind as well—and into the words of a people who were just beginning to find their voice—at last—in a new vernacular literature.

The Russian people had a rich oral tradition of storytelling in their vernacular language, but very little was written down until the late 18th century. Up until the late 17th century, the official, written language of Russian culture had remained Church Slavonic, the archaic language of the liturgy which was unintelligible to ordinary Russians. The law code of 1648 was the first book ever printed in vernacular Russian within Russia; and the written stories about Russia widely available inside Russia up until the early 19th century were for the most part recycled from formulaic lives of saints and monastic chronicles.

The only manuscript copy of the greatest of all early Russian epics, *The Lay of the Host of Igor*, had been destroyed in the Moscow fire of 1812, but Russian journals during Nicholas' reign were replete with new patriotic epics and historical novels written in the romantic style of Walter Scott. Perhaps the greatest historical novel ever written, Leo Tolstoy's *War and Peace,* was an epic focused on the conflict with Napoleon. But for Tolstoy, writing later in the 1860s, the real story of the victory lay neither in the official monuments nor in the military leadership of Imperial Russia—but in the mute, mysterious, almost impersonal power of the Russian people.

The story of the Russian people could never be told in stone. The heroic frescoes and bas reliefs of Nicholaevan Russia never depicted the ordinary, anonymous people of Russia whom the aristocrats and imperial bureaucrats of Petersburg hardly noticed and rarely spoke to. History, after the victory over Napoleon, became the heroic story of state-building Tsars and aristocrats in the majestic 12-volume *History of the Government of All Russia* by Nicholas Karamzin. This elegantly written, deeply conservative work continued to shape the historical imagination throughout Nicholas' reign.

Russian literature, in effect, was invented to reconnect the aristocracy with ordinary people who did not participate in the ritual life of St. Petersburg. With a desperation that intensified in the course of the 19th century, aristocratic Russian writers sought to discover in the unknown people all around them something real, possibly redemptive, but at least hopeful. Behind the stories they told was almost always the idealized memory of a childhood in a "nobleman's nest" in the countryside where they had lived happily with nature and with young serfs before moving into the more structured and artificial life of Petersburg and its 14-level hierarchy of power.

The man who showed the way and began to tell the story of ordinary Russia was Nicholas Gogol, an awkward and painfully shy lesser aristocrat with an unlikely provincial background. More than anyone else, he created Russian fiction. He brought the feel of the country back into the city, depicted the suffering human faces behind the facades of power, and provided for the great open-air theatre of Petersburg a dramatis personae that has permanently haunted the Russian imagination.

Gogol left the rural Ukraine of his youth for Petersburg on December 6, 1828, after celebrating the Feast of Saint Nicholas, his namesake and the patron saint of travellers. He was riding a troika, the simple, open carriage drawn by three horses that was all a minor aristocrat could afford. The 19-year-old boy wound his way through Ukraine, then known by its imperial name as "Little Russia," and Belorus (White Russia), lamenting that he never found a home he liked on the road.

His ride in the troika never really ended. He never did find a home, and no saint could protect him from burning what may have been his greatest work and starving himself to death 23 years later in Moscow.

The young Gogol en route to St. Petersburg had no clear idea what his profession would be. He wrote to his uncle that, if he ran out of resources, he could be "a good tailor, not a bad fresco painter, and capable of a few things in the culinary arts." But he was dazzled by the myth of the distant, shining capital. He had captured a glimpse of its provincial approximation on the estate of a distant relative where he had played bit parts in plays that were staged, and in some cases written, by his father.

He had written the same uncle in language at once baroque and romantic:

> Already from the most ancient times, from years beyond memory itself, I have been aflame with an unextinguishable ardor for making my life into something necessary for the good of the state, I have been boiling over to be of even the slightest service.

He was infatuated with the grandeur of Petersburg's imperial architecture, and found his first state job in the Department of Public Buildings of the Ministry of the Interior. But he lived in a dark apartment on a side street, and could not afford the expensive clothes needed to keep warm and maintain appearances in Petersburg. In 1829 he set off by sea to Lübeck and Hamburg, where he was enchanted by Gothic architecture. He soon fell sick, returned to Petersburg, and was promoted to the rank of collegiate assessor in the department of properties of the royal court. He took lessons in painting at the Academy of Beaux-Arts, tried out unsuccessfully for the Imperial Theatre, and began preparing lectures for the university on universal history.

Gogol in his early Petersburg years seemed almost a caricature of a restless romantic artist, wandering from medium to medium, job to job, in a youthful search to experience and accomplish something noble and grand. His earliest published literary efforts were poems on prototypical subjects of contemporary Western romanticism: a hymn to Italy in March and a longer saga *Hans Küchelbecker* in June of 1829. But he was also writing and rewriting an essay on architecture that clearly suggested that he would never fit harmoniously into Imperial Petersburg, and the culture of its self-satisfied aristocracy.

His essay of 1831, "On the Architecture of the Present Times," is a sustained lament for "the unrepeatable century of architecture" and the "greatness and genius" of both the Russian baroque and the Gothic West. They are now gone, forever. He begins:

> I always become sad when I look on the new buildings that are continuously being built, at which millions are thrown, and in which the eye of wonder rarely detects the outline of majesty, audacious imagination or even luxuriousness and dazzling, variegated decoration.

He dreams of building an immensely high tower "from which it would be possible to see everything in advance." But the only hope he finds for recovering architecture's "harmonic fusion of nature with art" lies in his final, fantastic thought that the decorations just then being hung from balconies and bridges in Petersburg might be the harbingers of a new "hanging architecture" whereby all Petersburg could be transformed "from the bottom up" into "a light net"—perhaps even detached from its earthly setting.

"Entire floors" of palaces and "audacious arches" would become "transparent iron scaffolding," and the "enor-

mous masses" of imperial buildings would be freed from
the "heavy columns" that hold them down. "Damask balconies" could "cheat the scales," and "winding around a
beautiful round tower," this "diaphanous veil" that once
was Petersburg would then "fly off together with it to
heaven.—What lightness, what aesthetic airiness our
homes would then have!"

There was little airiness in Gogol's real-life existence
in Petersburg—but clearly no limit to his imagination.
The freedom he sought in this fantasy was unrealizable in
architecture, but remained to be pursued in the new
medium of literature. Almost overnight, Gogol turned
his gaze away from castles in the air to reality on the
ground. He moved away from his side-street near St.
Isaac's to a roomier flat just off the long and bustling
Nevsky Prospect, turned from romantic poetry to realistic prose, and began to discover the forgotten people
who had been left out in the cold amidst the aristocratic
architecture of Petersburg.

He turned first for subject matter back to the Ukraine
of his childhood. Eight stories allegedly written by a bee-
keeper were published in two volumes as *Evenings on a
Farm near Dikanka* in 1831–32, followed by four more in
Mirgorod in 1835. Gogol fed the romantic appetite of the
city delicious word pictures of village life, strange images
from its rural folklore, and an overriding sense of the pet-
tiness and venality of provincial existence. In "Old World
Landowners," a fat couple simply eats incessantly, sits on
the porch and dies; in "How the Two Ivans Quarreled,"
two men with the same name quarrel endlessly about a
petty matter for 12 years; and, in the end, a weary witness
simply leaves in his troika.

Emaciated horses made unpleasant sounds as their hooves dragged through a mass of mud. The melancholy town gate where a crippled soldier was mending his uniform passed slowly by. Again the same meadows...wet crows and ravens, monotonous rain, a weeping sky...Life is boring in this world, gentlemen!

Gogol relieved the boredom that Petersburg aristocrats were feeling with stereotypical romantic themes borrowed from Germany. He introduced them instead to the wood sprites and nocturnal apparitions of Ukrainian folklore. The devil was alive and well in many different guises and shapes in the South, and Gogol's Ukrainian stories were an instant hit in the Russian North—winning for Gogol the supreme prize of friendship with Pushkin. Ukrainians sometimes wore pony tails, which were seen as a sign of savagery by Petersburg aristocrats, and Pushkin, after first meeting Gogol in 1831, referred to him as "the tufted one," *khokhol*, a mild ethnic slur that followed him to Moscow on his first visit there two years later. Gogol was lionized for providing a new source of provincial exoticism to rival that of the Caucasus, which had been celebrated in the poetry of Pushkin and Lermontov. But Ukrainian culture was closer to Russian, and Gogol brought into Petersburg from Ukraine something far more powerful than any of the themes from folklore used in his stories.

Gogol brought to Great Russia what might be described as the second stage of Little Russia. In the popular Ukrainian puppet theatre, the first stage on top always portrayed the official drama prescribed by the Church for the appointed feast day. This tradition derived from the Jesuit school dramas introduced to the Ukraine during its long period under Polish rule. This type of traveling theatrical presentation was generally referred to as the *Vertep* or "cave," which was represented as the site of Christ's birth in Orthodox icons.

But there was almost always a second stage—sometimes on a different level running along with the first, more often presented on the same stage in between the acts of the first or officially approved drama. On this stage, caricatured figures parodied the first stage and authority in general—expressing in popular vernacular the jaunty irreverence and idealized freedom of the Cossacks, a self-governing militia that guarded many outlying regions of the Russian empire. This second stage suggested that almost all foreigners and city people may really be devils in disguise. It was through a new version of this second stage that the carnival spirit depicted in Gogol's "Sorochinsky Fair" brought fresh animation into the dead architecture of Petersburg.

Gogol soon began to populate the theatrical city of Petersburg with characters suitable for an altogether new type of drama unlike either the tragedies or the comedies of the pre-existing aristocratic stage. He did his casting not in Rastrelli's palaces, but along the Nevsky Prospect. And he rarely looked for military heroes or true aristocrats. Nor did Gogol focus on the standard picture of an impractical, self-indulgent aristocrat who after Pushkin's *Eugene Onegin* became a stock character of Russian fiction: "the superfluous man." His stories about St. Petersburg (beginning with a volume *Arabesques* in 1835 and appearing in periodicals between 1836 and 1842) featured the minor clerks and struggling artists who lived with their apparitions on the side streets of a heartless city.

In a city built for parades rather than people, Gogol sought to find the faces behind the facades. He filled the empty courtyards of the great palaces with a new form of the satirical, second theatre that he remembered from his youth. He created the distinctively Russian type of drama that leads through laughter to tears and reached its zenith with the plays of Chekhov. But the faces he found were—like those in the Ukrainian puppet theatre—less than human. Gogol used an unprecedently large number of Russian and Ukrainian slang words to describe the human face. We remember his characters more by their distorted than by their attractive features. "The Nose," one of his most famous stories, depicts a nose separating from the face of a Petersburg official and leading a life of its own.

One of his most faceless characters became one of the most famous in all Russian literature: the minor clerk Akaky Akakevich in Gogol's "The Overcoat" of 1842. Akaky did not have a name ready for him at baptism, he was simply assigned his father's; and his pitiful life is focused entirely on getting a coat. When it is stolen, he dies, but comes back to take the coats off the backs of the mighty in Petersburg in posthumous revenge. The great Russian animator Yury Norstein has spent more than 20 years trying to bring this story to life. He explains that he was simply haunted by the pitiful question, usually asked only by children, that Akaky asks of his colleagues in the bureaucracy who are forever mocking him: "Why are you tormenting me?"

Gogol himself was tormented by Petersburg, and in 1836 he staged his great play, *The Inspector General*. He chose for his subject not the historic past as had Pushkin, but the imagined present—telling about a journey back to the countryside—as would his later magnum opus *Dead Souls*. The hero in both cases, however, is a trickster, and the people he meets in the provinces are awash in petty venality. The false inspector is a mindless talker; and, near the end, when the audience is laughing at the voluntary abasement of everyone before him, the mayor asks the question that Gogol wanted to pose to Russia itself: "Who are you laughing at? You are laughing at yourselves."

The immense success of this play merely deepened Gogol's own sense of personal failure. He left Petersburg later that year and remained basically on the road for the rest of his life. His sense of obligation to produce some great redemptive work for Russia was deepened by the premature death of Pushkin in a senseless duel in 1837. He had not only proclaimed Gogol to be his successor as the crown prince of Russian literature, he had also suggested the subject for Gogol's next—and last—major work, *Dead Souls*.

Gogol fled to Rome in search of the literary equivalent of a Gothic cathedral or a Rastrelli palace. He had taught medieval history for a brief period in Petersburg, lamenting that "as soon as the enthusiasm of the Middle Ages was extinguished...there was no longer anything truly great, gigantic" in the world. Perhaps, however, it would be possible to produce in the fresh medium of literature a Russian version of Dante's *Divine Comedy* in sunlit Italy itself.

Gogol's early years in Rome (1837–42) were the happiest of his life. He loved its food (especially spaghetti), its baroque splendor and classical ruins, and the sounds, sights, and smells of the surrounding countryside. Everything physical could be enjoyed and celebrated in the perpetual, Mediterranean springtime—even his elongated nose that had been the subject of jokes and torment in Petersburg:

> Sometimes I am seized by a frenzied desire to transform myself into one big nose whose nostrils would be as large as pails so that I could imbibe as much of the fragrance of spring as possible.

Rome was now "the homeland of my soul" where he would finally be able to pursue "the artistic-monastic life" and prove that "my journeys and withdrawals from the world have not been in vain."

He announced to his distant friends in Russia that he was beginning a work that would be "significant and great" and likened it, once again, to a work of architecture: "a gateway to that palace that arises within me."

But he was not building a structure, he was resuming his voyage—and it took him, in his imagination, back through the remotest, most monotonous expanses of the Russian countryside. His hero is not just the babbling Khlestakov of *The Inspector General*, but the more deeply corrupt Chichikov who plays on the endearing deformities of a host of petty provincial aristocrats to pursue his perverted task of buying up the titles to serfs who have died.

The various characters that Chichikov visits all have distinguishing physical characteristics which suggest different forms of venality, but Chichikov has no features at all. He is, in a way, the ultimate negation of the monastic ideal that Gogol was aspiring to live out. A monk has inner peace, radiates goodness and newness of life out to others, and finds his true self in stationary prayer in a fixed place. Chichikov is the emptiness inside Russia itself. He spreads infectious evil out to everyone with his unending search for the dead. He is forever on the road.

Gogol was himself travelling all over western Europe as he was writing *Dead Souls*; but the more he saw of the West, the more his imagination focused on Russia. His reveries of deliverance were no longer castles in the air, but roads on the ground in Russia itself. With a touch of the masochism that recurs throughout his work—and in much of subsequent Russian literature—Gogol rhapsodizes about the muddy, crooked roads of Old Russia— and about the troika that ordinary Russians use to pass over them.

Like the facades covering the empty courtyards of Petersburg, the main characters masking the emptiness of Russia itself literally fade into thin air in Gogol's fevered imagination. In a new stage direction that he wrote in 1842 for actors playing the lead role in *The Inspector General*, Gogol writes: "Khlestakov is a phantasmagorical figure who, like an embodied fraud, vanishes into thin air with his troika."

In the same year, at the very end of the first part of *Dead Souls*, Gogol expands this image into a metaphor for Russia itself—called once again by its ancient, sanctified name of Rus.

And art not thou, Rus, rushing on like a spirited troika that none can pass? The road smokes with smoke under thee; bridges thunder; everything lags and is left behind....Rus, whither art thou rushing? Give an answer. She gives no answer. The harness bells dissolve into wondrous ringing. The air is shattered into shreds, it roars and turns into wind. Everything on earth flies by...other nations and governments step aside and give the road over to thee.

The road for Gogol in the last ten years of his life seemed to lead back to the traditional Russian values of the Orthodox Church and a hierarchical society. He devoted himself mainly to moralistic essays and letters that enraged liberals who had previously admired his work and perplexed conservatives who had previously enjoyed his company. He never completed any major work of fiction from 1842 to 1852, leaving behind only a few fragments of the second part of *Dead Souls*. He seemed—like Leo Tolstoy later—to have renounced art for moralism at the very zenith of his artistic achievements. Gogol become even more than Tolstoy a deeply lonely man. Yet, in truth, he was only moving into a deeper and more desperate phase of his continuing search for redemption through art. And, in his last years, his troika was blazing trails into the Russian future.

Without a family, without a home, Gogol had to find a place where he could feel at home. He turned to tradition precisely because of the rigid sense of place presented both on the icon screen and in the hierarchical society of Russia. Status in society was not important, since all stations on earth are equidistant from God. But how does one approach divinity from a world of dead souls? In his never-completed Part II, Gogol sought to turn human tragedy into a divine comedy: to begin moving out from the corrupt inferno he had depicted in Part I through purgatory to paradise.

His place was no longer in Rome, nor Jerusalem, nor anywhere even in Great or Little Russia—though he voyaged through all these places in his late years. His true home was in Rus, Holy Russia as it is sometimes called— more a spiritual ideal than a physical place. At the end of his *Diary of a Madman*, Gogol's terrified hero cries out from the asylum for a troika to "carry me away from this world." And in a lacerating final plea, he cries out, "Mother, save your wretched son...Hold me, a poor waif, in your arms. There is no room for him in this world."

Now, from Rome, Gogol was crying out to Mother Russia, *Matushka Rus*, to find some room for him in her world. And in his fevered imagination, Gogol seeks it in the deep interior of Russia—in what he called the *glush'*, which suggests some dark, solitary, and silent place of indeterminate location.

The fragments that have survived from Part II of *Dead Souls* begin with a fantastic image of Rus in which nature blends into architecture. Mountains "meander" for "more than a thousand miles...like the giant rampart of some endless fortress." A tableau includes every kind of tree, wood carvings around windows and balconies on peasant huts, and red roofs on manor houses—all topped by a giant church with five domes, each with a glorious hand-worked cross "so that the gold shone from afar as if it were suspended in air, not attached to anything." Looking at it all from on high and through its reflection on the water, Gogol twice cries out "Lord, how spacious it is here."

Into this capacious, imaginary world, Gogol attempts

to introduce a more exemplary group of characters than appeared in Part I. He even tries to portray some positive development in Chichikov himself—and suggests in a letter that he hoped to depict the conversion of Chichikov to a life of total service to others "with the direct participation of the Tsar himself in this conversion." But Gogol successively destroyed each of his two manuscripts for Part II, and the passages that have survived do not depict characters that are nearly as memorable as the vivid caricatures of Part I. Chichikov seems merely to have wandered into a "moral no man's land" with some doubts about his mission, but no new sense of direction. Gogol's last description of his last hero is that of a man who is no longer "the old Chichikov," but simply "the ruins of the old Chichikov." Once again, the image is architectural.

> The inner state of his soul might be compared to a demolished building—torn down so that a new one could be built from it. But the new one has not yet been started, because the definitive plan has not yet come from the architect, and the workers are left bewildered.

Gogol admits defeat in what was to become a central preoccupation of modern Russian literature: the search for a "positive hero." He cannot portray perfection, the moralist in him now argues, because he has not yet become perfect enough himself. He had failed to create a positive hero because:

> You cannot invent them out of your head. Until you become like them yourself, until you acquire a few

good qualities by your perseverance and strength of character, everything you produce by your pen will be nothing but carrion...

And so, the great writer burned a large section of what he had written for Part II in 1845 and set out on a last journey to find the faith that could make him whole. He went on a pilgrimage to Jerusalem, but found himself no different after an all night vigil by the Holy Sepulchre. "It is as if I made this pilgrimage to prove and to see with my own eyes the barren nature of my heart." His only happiness seemed to come from gathering wild flowers in Galilee, which reminded him of Russia. He wrote a friend:

> Russia is your monastery...You must go all over Russia...In the journey itself you will be presented with heroic Christian deeds that you will never find in a monastery itself.

Gogol traveled widely in the south of Russia and Ukraine during his last years, and showed a special interest in a new kind of monastery that had suddenly grown up in a wooded region south of Moscow. It was a new "desert," the Optyna Pustyn, which had developed a legendary reputation for curing mental illness and providing spiritual counsel.

Gogol's Slavophile friends were frequent visitors; but Gogol was the first great writer to make pilgrimages there, in the summer of 1850 and again in the fall of 1851, for confession and counseling in this new version of the oldest form of Christian monastery: a hermitage for desert fathers.

Optyna was, in a sense, Gogol's last place for rest and refreshment by the side of the long road that was his life. It was one of the centers in which the ascetic tradition was being revived after Catherine the Great had confiscated the property and undermined the independent authority of the older monasteries. Optyna was said to have been named for a forest thief named Opta, who was miraculously converted in the 14th century and became a hermit. In the 1820s, it suddenly blossomed as a center for spiritual elders who revived the austere monastic tradition of the legendary Opta's time—and also provided spiritual guidance to lay people.

The prophecy of these elders carried special authority because their words came after long periods of purifying silence. In the words of Yeats: "Speech after long silence, it is right." Talkative writers longed for a few words of wisdom from those who were not part of their own endless conversations that somehow always ended in gossip and bickering. One such prophetic elder of the early 19th century, Seraphim of Sarov, left behind a prophecy—discovered only much later—that Russia would pass through a revolutionary century of totally rejecting God before returning to Christ. Dostoevsky's Father Zosima in the *Brothers Karamazov* is a model portrayal of the spiritual *starets* or elder.

The building in which Gogol received counsel was a curious architectural hybrid. It was called a *skit*, the name derived from wandering and usually given for a remote hermitage. But it was located in the center of the monastery itself. It was made entirely of wood and rather small, but it was built in the neo-classical Petersburg style designed for stone and stucco. Just as monastic Muscovy had transposed wooden architecture into stone, so now aristocratic Russia was turning stone forms back into wood. Every attempt, it seemed, to turn aristocratic Russia back to the monastic culture of old was plagued by such incongruities. The only contribution of the aristocratic era to the mother Monastery of St. Sergius was a baroque bell tower that dominated the skyline but destroyed the integrity of that great medieval ensemble.

Gogol sought out spiritual guides during his final years in Moscow. The last one, Father Matthew, was unable to halt (and is sometimes credited with encouraging) the ascetic regime that led to Gogol's death on February 21, 1852.

Gogol's journey had in fact ended ten days earlier. On February 7, the first Sunday in Lent, he took communion for the last time and went to a hospital to visit a celebrated Holy Fool, one of the wandering, ascetic prophets who were exercising renewed influence on the Russian imagination. Gogol never went in. On February 9 he called for a priest to deliver last rites, but he rose to attend vespers on February 11. At about three o'clock in the morning on February 12, he took the manuscript for his second try at completing *Dead Souls* out of his bedroom-study into a small adjacent room and burned it.

The only witness was his illiterate, 15-year-old peasant servant. Beginning on February 13, he stopped both eating and conversation with his friends, who pleaded with him to live and tried many medical treatments—including a final grotesque act worthy of Gogol's own prose: bleeding through the nose with leeches on his deathbed. His last, delirious spoken words were "a ladder...

quickly, a ladder"—clearly summoning up the image portrayed on the icon of John of the Ladder, where the pilgrim's struggle for salvation is depicted as the perilous ascent up a ladder to heaven. His last written words were from St. Matthew's gospel, composed in large, child-like letters with a trembling hand: "Unless you become like a little child, you shall not enter into the kingdom of heaven."

Gogol's only memorial museum in Russia today is the half-hidden three rooms of the house in which he died, which is now largely given over to other uses. Outside is a mournful and meditative statue of Gogol seated—far less visible than the stereotypical standing statue of a heroic writer that Soviet authorities put in its place for public viewing in Moscow.

Gogol never seems to have found the "heroic Christian deeds" in Rus that could have led from his inferno of the dead to the paradise of eternal life. Nor did he seem to find the peace that passes understanding that his own faith might have provided. But the last essay in his *Selected Passages from a Correspondence with Friends* of 1847 contains one of the most disquietingly beautiful essays ever written on the central feast of the Orthodox Church—the Easter that he never lived to celebrate in 1852.

At one level, his "Shining Resurrection" is simply an extended, somewhat nationalistic hymn of self-praise, commending Russia for feeling Easter more deeply than other nations. The 19th century has produced a new type of man who "is prepared to embrace all humanity as a brother, yet will not embrace his own brother." The devil speaks now "without masks" and creates "pride of the mind." Yet God is still "ready to throw out a ladder from heaven and extend a hand to help him climb up." The cry of "Christ is Risen" that the priest proclaims at midnight is taken up by "the booming sounds of all-ringing bells that rejoice and resonate over the entire earth" telling people that "wherever they are, they will awake."

Gogol seems to echo the old Muscovite idea that sanctity radiates out as far as the bells can be heard; and the Russian text itself rings with sonorous repetitions (*Guly . . . gudyat i gulyat . . . gde budyat, tam razbudyat*). But Gogol personally seems to have identified at the end of his life more with the existential anguish of modern man haunted by unbelief on the eve of Easter:

> Life becomes more and more callous. Everything gets smaller and more shallow; and there rises up before all one gigantic image of boredom which every day reaches new enormity. All is deafness. The grave is everywhere. Lord! How empty and terrifying everything in your world has become!

The petty demons and boredom of provincial Russia seem, at the end, to have claimed the very man who had best described them. Gogol's cry of anguish in his "Shining Resurrection" is strikingly similar to the lacerating final words at the end of his "How the Two Ivans Quarreled." Neither the architecture that had drawn him away from the provinces to Petersburg nor the writing that he had done on his subsequent journey had produced the saving work for Russia that he had dreamed of. He could not achieve artistic perfection without becoming perfect himself. And even worship would not

1. Andrei Rublev, *Spas* (The Savior), 1420s, Tretyakov Gallery, Moscow. An icon showing the softened expression and slightly elongated form of the distinctive image of Christ painted by the greatest of all monastic icon painters for the central panel of the icon screen for the Cathedral of the Assumption in Zvenigorod. Rescued from a shed for firewood in 1918.

2. The Vladimir Mother of God, first half of the 12th century, Tretyakov Gallery, Moscow. A Byzantine icon brought from Constantinople to Kiev in the 1130s, to Vladimir in 1155 (whence its name), to Moscow briefly in 1395 when Tamerlane was threatening, and to Moscow permanently in 1480 to the Cathedral of the Assumption in the Kremlin until 1918.

3. Theophanes the Greek, The Transfiguration, early 15th century, Tretyakov Gallery, Moscow. Following the Gospel account (Matt. 17: 1–9), this icon was originally painted for the Cathedral of the Transfiguration in Pereyaslavl-Zalesk. It shows Christ's disciples dazzled by his appearance on Mt. Tabor transfigured in pure white. St. Paul on the left puts his hands in front of his face; Sts. James and John fall away with a rhythmic motion later echoed in paintings of an altogether different nature. Since icons tell the whole story of a saint or sacred event, we also see in the inserts on either side a depiction of the saints climbing down the mountain—and, on either side of Christ, Elijah and Moses, with whom he conversed, and angels in the clouds above showing each of them the way.

4. Theophanes the Greek, St. Macarius, 1378. A fresco by the Greek
mentor and collaborator of Rublev in the Cathedral of the Transfiguration
of the Redeemer in Novgorod. This ascetic, fourth-century monastic pioneer in the Egyptian desert was especially revered in the Russian North.

5. Andrei Rublev, The Old Testament Trinity, 1422–27, Tretyakov Gallery, Moscow. This icon depicts a simplified version of the Old Testament event that prefigured the central Christian mystery of the Holy Trinity: the appearance of three pilgrims to Abraham (Gen. 18: 1–13—as sung in the Orthodox liturgy: "Blessed Abraham, thou who hast received the divine one-in-three"). Both the outer and the inner contours of the two flanking figures echo the "inverse perspective" created by the communion chalice, which is thrust out at the viewer. The beginning of a V-shape formed by the white table can be completed only outside the picture itself—with the lines converging at the point where the viewer is standing. Icons—unlike most Western religious paintings—have no natural perspective or vanishing point inside the picture. The viewer is kept at a distance from divine mysteries, yet is invited to contemplate this ultimate model of community (the Russian *sobornost*) by the central figure of Christ wearing the red robe of martyrdom and pointing towards the cup. Painted for the central Trinity Cathedral of the Monastery of St. Sergius and the Holy Trinity in Sergiev Posad, this icon was deemed so perfect that it was prescribed to be the exact model for all future paintings on this subject by the Church Council of 1551.

6. St. George and the Dragon, early 15th century, Novgorod School, Tretyakov Gallery, Moscow. Both the sun emitting rays on the shield and the anatomically exaggerated white horse show the continuing influence of the pre-Christian sun god in the Russian North.

7. Interior view of *nebo* ceiling, 1761, Intercession Church at Village of Liadiny, Arkhangelsk Province. The inner ceilings of old Russian wooden churches often portrayed an image of Christ or, as here, the Holy Trinity as a sun radiating out rays of sanctity through heavenly creatures to the disciples and apostles—providing the equivalent in wood to the frescoes that adorned comparable space in stone churches. The original *nebo* at Kizhi still exists, but has not yet been fully restored and placed back in the church. Photograph by William Brumfield.

8. Transfiguration Church, 1714, at Kizhi. Built without nails from wood hewn only with an axe, this magnificent church on a remote island in a northern lake has onion domes—yet a stately unity in its tent-like structure. Its jagged shape is often compared to that of the fir tree from which its wood was largely hewn. Photograph by William Brumfield.

9. Dionysius, The Journey of the Three Wise Men, 1502, Ferapontov. This fresco from the Cathedral of the Nativity of the Virgin illustrates the ninth canticle in the 25-hymn cycle in praise of the Virgin known as Akathistos.

10. Vasily Surikov, *Boyaryna Morozova*, 1881–87, Tretyakov Gallery, Moscow. Like so many of these vast historical canvases, Surikov made an immense number of sketches both of the overall composition and of almost every individual figure. Morozova was a passionate Old Believer, who wrote some of the most moving letters of Old Russia from her imprisonment. In the lower right a holy fool is blessing her.

11. If the painted figure of Morozova above shows her making the two-fingered sign of the cross characteristic of the Old Believers, the illustration from a typical tract of the Old Believers contrasts their own traditional dress and eight-pointed cross with the short coat, shaven face, and four-pointed Latin cross that they felt had corrupted the Russian Church with Western secularism.

12. Simon Ushakov, The Planting of the Tree of the Russian State, 1668,
Tretyakov Gallery, Moscow. The icon shows the tree of the Russian State
being watered by the first Prince of Moscow, Ivan Kalita, and Metropolitan
Peter, the first head of the church to reside in Moscow. The spiritual world
of the icon has been broken up by a painter already skilled in lifelike
portraiture. The Vladimir Mother of God is represented in a naturalistic
manner and surrounded with the figures of twenty Russian church and state
leaders.

13. The Battle between Novgorod and Suzdal, late 15th century, Novgorod
School, Tretyakov Gallery, Moscow. This is the earliest known icon depicting a purely internal political event within Russia: the successful resistance
of Novgorod against a siege by the rival principality, Suzdal, in 1169. The
scene at the top shows an icon of the Virgin being carried for protection
into the Novgorod Kremlin. The middle panel shows the negotiations of
the three-man teams being broken off by the Suzdalians shooting arrows
that are aimed at—but miraculously stopped by—the icon. The final panel
shows Russian saints leading the Novgorodians out of the gates to vanquish
the blasphemous Suzdalians.

14. The Church Militant, mid-16th century, Tretyakov Gallery, Moscow. This icon from the Cathedral of the Assumption in the Moscow Kremlin depicts the procession of the righteous from Sodom to the New Jerusalem, led by the Archangel Michael on a winged horse. It also illustrates the mixture of secular with sacred themes. Painted shortly after the fall of the Muslim Tatar city of Kazan to Ivan the Terrible, the icon mixes Russian leaders in with the saints in the long line of horsemen. The Archangel himself is looking back at the figure of Ivan immediately behind him. The composition seems to suggest that Sodom is Kazan, and Moscow the New Jerusalem.

15. Kazimir Malevich, *Red Cavalry*, 1928–32, Russian Museum, St. Petersburg. This painting represents the attempt late in the life of the great modernist painter to draw on the old iconographic image of a line of horsemen as liberators in support of the Soviet system during the traumatic transformations of collectivization and forced industrialization of the first five-year plan period.

16. Deposition from the Cross (above), last quarter of 16th century, Novgorod School, Tretyakov Gallery, Moscow. Anatomical exaggeration underscores the basic meaning of the icon. As pointed out by Camilla Gray, the striking curvilinear pattern of the lines in this icon were echoed in the semi-abstract painting (right) of a totally different subject by the modernist artist Vladimir Tatlin, *Composition from a Nude*, 1913, Tretyakov Gallery, Moscow.

17. In the detail above from The Transfiguration (see illustration 3 for a view of the full icon) St. Paul on the left puts his hands in front of his face; Sts. James and John fall away. In the otherwise totally different painting at the right, *Playing Boys* (Kuzma Petrov-Vodkin, 1911, Russian Museum, St. Petersburg), the hiding of eyes and the movements of the figures suggest unconscious borrowing from these classic iconographic forms as well as from contemporary artists like Matisse.

18. Circular wooden image of a sun placed on the prow of a ship in the Russian North. Personal photograph of the author.

19. Bartolomeo Rastrelli, Palace exterior, Tsarskoe Selo, 1748–56.
Photograph by William Brumfield.

20. Bartolomeo Rastrelli, The Great Palace and Samson Fountain, north facade, Peterhof, 1714–52. Completely destroyed in World War II, both of these imperial palaces were priority reconstruction projects which painstakingly re-created their original majesty and lent a kind of paternity to the grandiose ambitions of the late Soviet period. Photograph by William Brumfield.

21. Karl Briullov, *The Last Day of Pompeii*, 1830–33, Russian Museum, St. Petersburg. This was the first of the enormous 19th-century Russian paintings that were thought to have profound, if not prophetic, significance. Nationalistic conservatives saw it as a depiction of divine retribution against Western decadence. Radicals were excited that—in the words of Briullov's biographer, E.N. Atsarkina—for the first time a historical depiction in Russia was focused on "the drama of the people, and not the personal fate of a hero." Gogol in 1834 expressed his "rapture" at the appearance of such a "complete universal creation" in which "sculpture... is converted into painting and then rises still higher and is infused with some kind of secret music." Gogol likened this painting to an opera in which "painting, poetry and music" are all brought together. The painting was, in fact, partly inspired by the now-forgotten opera of Giovanni Pacini, *L'ultimo giorno di Pompeii* (1824), and this canvas became, in turn, a favorite of later composers seeking to write distinctively Russian opera.

22. Alexander Ivanov, *Portrait of Gogol*, 1841, Russian Museum, St. Petersburg.

23a. Alexander Ivanov, *Appearance of Christ to the People*, final variant, 1837-57, Tretyakov Gallery, Moscow.

23b. Details, *Appearance of Christ to the People*, early variant, left, Russian Museum, St. Petersburg, and final variant, right. Ivanov placed Gogol "closest to Christ" in all his mature versions of this painting. Whereas Gogol in the upper right-hand corner of the painting is shown turning away from Christ in the earlier version, he faces him in the last and largest version of this much labored painting.

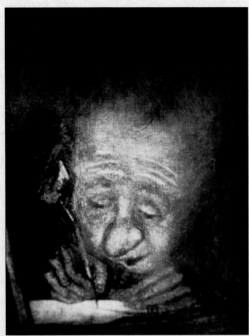

24. Yury Norstein, Akaky Akakevich, the little clerk from Nicholas Gogol's "The Overcoat." He uses a unique style of animation based on two-dimensional puppets with multiple moving parts. He echoes the tradition of icon painting by letting the face and hands convey the essential story. Photograph by the artist from the animated version of this story on which he has been working for 20 years.

25. Ilya Repin, *Haulers on the Volga*, 1870–73, Russian Museum, St. Petersburg. As with so many major canvases of this period, Repin's work was the result of a large number of sketches. Revolutionaries were inspired by the image of the young boy who was thought to be looking beyond the toil towards some distant liberation.

26. Ivan Kozlovsky as the Holy Fool, in *Boris Godunov*, Bolshoi Theatre, 1954. From the collection of the Bakhrushin Theatre Museum, Moscow.

27. Ilya Repin, *Portrait of Musorgsky*, 1881, Tretyakov Gallery, Moscow. Painted in a hospital just a few days before Musorgsky died, this is the portrait which Shostakovich, in many ways the 20th-century perpetuator of Musorgsky's musical tradition, kept on his writing desk while composing his own music.

28. Ilya Repin, *Ivan the Terrible and His Son*, 1885, Tretyakov Gallery, Moscow. This painting commemorates the event on November 16, 1581, when Ivan struck his son—his namesake and heir—with a staff and killed him. Repin shows Ivan clinging to his dying son, who is rendered in a manner to suggest Christ. Ivan's severing of the line of succession created a crisis of legitimacy and led to Russia's original "Time of Troubles."

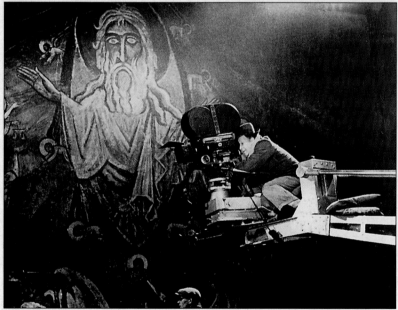

29. Sergei Eisenstein, *Ivan the Terrible, Part III*. These stills, kindly provided by Naum Kleiman from his personal collection, depict what would have been a climactic scene in the suppressed third part of this epic film: the conversation with God that Ivan directs to the fresco. The second illustration shows Eisenstein filming this scene.

30. Nadezhda Mandelstam and Varlam Shalamov, photograph taken by the author in 1967. The author was privileged to participate in a number of remarkable evening discussions held in the kitchen of Nadezhda Mandelstam, widow of the great poet Osip Mandelstam, who died in Stalin's gulag. She is pictured here with Varlam Shalamov, who wrote some of the most powerful, yet serene, literary descriptions of the gulag experience. He was a living legend in the post-Stalin USSR. Almost every bone in his body had been broken, but he miraculously survived seventeen years in the ultimate death camp of the Soviet system in Kolyma, where three million perished. These two—along with Alexander Solzhenitsyn and Andrei Sakharov— kept alive the conscience of Russia during the long period before the Soviet system began to disintegrate.

31. The painter Elena Fradkina, the sister-in-law of Nadezhda Mandelstam, is shown here at the opening in late 1966 of the first exhibition of her modernist paintings that was ever permitted in the Soviet Union. She is photographed with the author's two daughters, Anne and Susan, ages six and eight, who were then attending Russian schools. At the opening, Fradkina identified herself with them and their generation, saying that she felt herself to be just four years old, since she had been able to have access to her own artistic legacy only for the last four years. Photograph by the author.

Fradkina had designed sets for the Kamerny Theatre of Alexander Tairov, which was famed for the aesthetic elegance of its apolitical productions. Stalin shut it down in 1949. Tairov had said as early as 1920: "A propagandistic theatre after a revolution is like mustard after a meal."

perfect him—he seemed to say in his last work *Reflections on the Divine Liturgy*—because priests themselves were not perfect.

In his last years, Gogol entertained the hope that the great and terrifying space of Russia might somehow be enclosed—and a positive message conveyed—through the original art of Christian Russia: painting.

Amidst the visual beauty of Rome, Gogol came to feel that painting was superior to statuary and all other forms of plastic art, because "its borders are wider; it includes in itself the whole world . . . the linking of man with nature." As he gave up on completing his own great work of literature, he transferred his hopes for some new and redemptive work of art for Russia to his close friend in Rome, the painter Alexander Ivanov.

Ivanov seems to have seen himself as the man who would at last bring the artistic perfection of Renaissance Italy singlehandedly into Orthodox Russia. His father had been the leading academic painter in Petersburg, but Ivanov had fled "that city which has no character" in 1830 for Rome, where he studied the great works of Leonardo, Raphael, and Michelangelo and used them as models for a series of classical canvases on biblical themes. He also sketched Daumier-like, black-and-white Roman street scenes and became the first Russian painter extensively to paint outdoor scenes directly from nature in the open air.

Ivanov was fascinated by the giant canvas, "The Last Day of Pompeii," that Karl Briullov had spent six years painting in Rome and finally exhibited in 1833 (see illustration 21). It seemed to illustrate the decline and fall of the decadent West in an exaggerated and melodramatic way. Ivanov set off to produce an equally gigantic canvas—but one that would illustrate the rise of the positive Christian alternative in the East in a realistic and classical way.

He chose as his subject the first appearance of Christ to the people after his baptism in the Jordan River. This was the decisive moment in human history. It had been completely overlooked in the older iconography—but could be presented in a new way that would depict the event as it actually happened and combine all the best techniques of both the Italian Renaissance art that Russians had never previously known and the new realistic techniques Ivanov was experimenting with in Rome. This painting would show the transfigured faces of those who first looked at the Savior—and by extension would transform the faces and save the lives of all who looked on the painting.

The painting could be an instrument for converting 19th-century man, Ivanov believed, because it would be produced by a prophetic artist who "leads his life in a truly monastic way . . . praying every minute"—and who "by the will of God begins to rework the very nature of man. I know this and in part have even begun to experience it."

In his search for authenticity, Ivanov drew up some 600 sketches over 25 years, visiting courtrooms, synagogues, public baths, remote country regions of Italy, ancient mosaics in Jerusalem, and museums in Rome—all in search of the right face for both the historical Jesus and the motley crowd to whom he had first appeared in the Jordanian desert.

Gogol was fascinated with this megalomanic project;

and belief in the redemptive power of this picture grew after Nicholas I made a special visit to Ivanov's studio during his trip to Rome in December 1845. Ivanov likened the Tsar's visit to the Second Coming of Christ and began planning a secret project for a temple in Red Square that would feature a giant fresco of the Holy Lands with Nicholas I in the center as the new Messiah.

Beyond their shared turn to messianic nationalism, Ivanov and Gogol each sought not just to create a new Christian art, but to become himself a kind of Christ. When shown some humorous drawings Ivanov repressed his laughter and after a long silence simply said "Christ never smiled." And Ivanov piled on himself yet another massive project: the full depiction of the Old Testament prophecy and New Testament account of the life of Christ—completing 246 remarkable drawings.

Ivanov returned to Russia in 1858, six years after Gogol died, only to see his giant canvas met with bewilderment and indifference and to die broken-hearted shortly thereafter. Even more than Gogol, Ivanov had lost his faith in his quest for redemptive art, and the people to whom his distant Christ appears hardly notice him in their preoccupation with worldly concerns. Scornfully referred to as "the disappearance of Christ into the people," the painting is dominated by the figure of John the Baptist as befits a prophetic art. But Ivanov made a final gesture to his fellow truth-seeker in Rome. He painted Gogol as the person closest to Christ in his canvas—hiding his face in the next-to-last version of the painting, but facing his Savior in the final version (see illustrations 23a and 23b).

By the time of Ivanov's death, his would-be Messiah

Nicholas I had been humiliated by England and France in the Crimean War (1853–56) and had been succeeded by the reform-minded Alexander II. The troika was beginning to give way to the railroad. The first small railroad in Russia connected Petersburg and Tsarskoe Selo. The new Moscow Station on the Nevsky Prospect in St. Petersburg provided the capital with one of its last great baroque facades. After Alexander II, in 1862, freed the peasants of Russia from the bondage of serfdom which had treated them as property, steam engines began to bring in rural workers for the new factories. A mass culture was coming into being.

Gogol changed the basic direction of Russian literature from the poetic perfection and Shakespearean sweep of Pushkin into the anguished striving and ideological-religious direction of Dostoevsky. Gogol imparted to Russian culture the belief that art should save and not merely entertain his countrymen.

Gogol never created a positive hero, but in the surviving few fragments of the second part of *Dead Souls*, he presents a surprisingly liberal image of landowners trying to institute reforms. So, in a way, his concern for ordinary people and for mixing laughter with the tears of real life can be said to anticipate the struggle in Russia today for a "civilized" and "normal" society of moderation.

But Gogol was in no way a normal person or writer. No subsequent regime has felt entirely comfortable in attempting to adopt and domesticate his legacy. There are few monuments dedicated to Gogol despite the monument-mania of modern Russia. Yet everyone wants to identify himself with the cleansing power of his writings. Even Stalin, who had destroyed every genuine satirist he could find in the Soviet Union, called at his last Communist Party Congress in late 1952 for the creation of new Gogols.

Gogol left an extraordinarily rich, essentially three-part legacy to Russian history and culture. First was his influence on the social criticism of Tsarist Russia. His satire of provincial backwardness and official pomposity did a great deal to delegitimize the very political and social order that he ultimately defended with great passion. He was long seen as a partial source of inspiration for the very revolution he sought to avoid. Dying before there was a revolutionary movement, he nonetheless turned the gaze of art onto social reality and took the side of the forgotten and suffering people of Petersburg. One of Gogol's biographers, David Magarshack, quotes Vasily Rozanov as saying that:

> Russia was, or at least appeared to be, a "monumental," "majestic," "great power," yet Gogol walked over these real or imaginary "monuments" with his thin weak feet and crushed them all, so that not a trace of them remained.

Second was Gogol's belated but powerful influence on the Russian religious revival that began early in this century and has resumed vigorously since the fall of Communism. People have been moved not so much by the moralistic writings of his last years as by his personal example of searching for faith in a modern environment—and by the Christian humanism that underlies his art and makes us feel compassion and some affection even for the most caricatured figures in *Dead Souls*.

Finally, and perhaps most important, was Gogol's impact on the dissident subculture of the Soviet era. He was seen as having penetrated from the real to the more real—even to the surreal. He was seen as a force for promoting subversive change. Andrei Siniavsky, one of the most celebrated literary prisoners of the Brezhnev era, wrote an entire book about Gogol while in confinement, *In the Shadow of Gogol* (1975). Gogol's world provided an effective platform for dissident opposition. In a time when people were often behaving like puppets, puppets began to acquire the attributes of people. The leading composer of the period, Rodion Shchedrin, produced for the Bolshoi Theatre in Moscow an operatic version of *Dead Souls* (1972) which divided the stage between an upper level where the troika rode on and a lower level where petty venality reigned.

In post-Communist Russia, Gogol continues to inspire those on the cutting artistic edge. Eduard Bersudsky's Barrel Organ Theatre brings grotesque, faintly comic machines into Petersburg, reminiscent of the petty demons from the Ukraine that Gogol introduced to Petersburg through his literature. And the cruelty and corruption of Russia's indestructible government bureaucracy is countered even today through new versions of old Gogolian works. A new production of *The Inspector General* at the Stanislavsky Theatre ends by breaking up the light on the stage and reflecting it back to the audience with a host of mirrors. A clown like Slava Polunin bring tears and a touch of pure Gogolian absurdity into the stereotypical routine of a circus act that might otherwise only make us laugh.

Gogol once tried to explain that laughter itself had

been his positive hero, but he never outgrew the fears and tears of a country boy always homesick in cities. He was unable even to smile at the end of his long journey.

No one illustrates better than Gogol the recurrent cycle of borrow, innovate, and destroy that new art media experience in Russia. His first major work was in title, form, and content a piece of pure poetic borrowing from German romanticism. He initially fled to Germany when it was badly received, and he then turned to other finished Western models: E.T.A. Hoffmann's tales of the grotesque and eventually Dante's *Divine Comedy*—even entitling his *Dead Souls* a *Poema.*

But no one produced more strikingly original literary innovations than Gogol. His cascade of non sequiturs, his florid language, and, above all, the intense overload of metaphysical searching that he placed on his artistic quest—all made him an innovator of genius even in an already well-worked-over art form.

And no one experienced a more tragic breakup of art and breakdown of self than Gogol in his late years. Gogol set the pattern for many future writers of desperately trying to write the Russian version of our "great American novel"—yet ultimately destroying his own work and even himself.

Most important of all for the future of Russia—even today—is the indelible message that Gogol left behind with the witness of his own short life: that the search for truth is more noble than the exercise of power. Being on the road is more important than being in a palace; and the greatest threats may come from impostors on that road like Khlestakov or Chichikov.

If there was a positive hero out there in what one critic

has called "the suffering languor of the Russian spaces," it was the little people like Akaky Akakevich in Gogol's "Overcoat" who will somehow be vindicated. All of Russian literature, any number of people have said, comes out from under Gogol's overcoat. In Yury Norstein's animated re-creation of this one short story, each figure in each episode is an artistic, two-dimensional puppet with multiple moving parts. The movement of fingers has a lifelike quality; the expression of faces, a sad beauty; and the representation of Akaky Akakevich, a special, childlike quality (see illustration 24). Like Gogol's own lifework, Norstein's is still uncompleted.

Pushkin created the Russian literary language and the model for poetic perfection to which Russian writers have continually returned to admire and emulate in the modern age. But Gogol created the supercharged universe of ideological prose fiction that would dazzle the world within a generation of his death.

Gogol had sought not so much to *write* as to *do* something big for Russia: a *podvig* or heroic deed like those of Russia's original saints and warriors. In one of his longest short stories, "Taras Bulba," he had described the implausible heroism of Cossack warriors; and he died imitating, in effect, a monastic preparation for sainthood through fasting and self-denial.

Writers in the generation after Gogol continued and in some ways completed his work—giving the seemingly finished form of the European novel a breadth and depth it had never attained before. But there was almost always a haunting Gogolian echo at the end.

A new breadth came with Tolstoy's epic novel *War and Peace*, but Tolstoy like Gogol eventually renounced art at the height of his powers and tried to become a moral teacher for the Russian people. A new depth came with Dostoevsky's dramatic penetration into the human psyche, but he, like Gogol, created his greatest masterpiece, *The Brothers Karamazov*, as only the first part of a projected redemptive trilogy: *The Life of a Great Sinner*. Both Dostoevsky and Tolstoy followed Gogol's example and visited the elders at Optyna Pustyn.

Dostoevsky deepened the effort of Gogol's final years to bring modern man back to Orthodox Christianity, to see through the suffering of ordinary people a "God-bearing" mission for Russia. In his *Idiot*, he introduces a Christ figure into a contemporary setting, and in *Crime and Punishment* and *The Possessed* he portrays the murderous results of modern man's arrogation of God-like powers to himself.

Tolstoy amplified on a titanic scale the example Gogol had set of renouncing art altogether for moral pedagogy. Unlike Gogol, Tolstoy had finished his major life's work (not only *War and Peace*, but *Anna Karenina*) before renouncing art; also unlike Gogol, Tolstoy rejected both church and state. He became in effect a peaceful anarchist, preaching nonresistance to evil and writing simple moralistic tales for the peasantry. But in a deeper sense he followed the Gogolian path—destroying the writing he might have done during the last 30 years of his life and, at the end, destroying himself. Though he was of higher aristocratic rank than Gogol and had the beautiful country home and loving family that Gogol never found, Tolstoy left it all and died literally on the road, in a railroad station not far from Optyna. His sister was a nun in the convent that grew up alongside Optyna, and

Tolstoy might in fact have been heading there for one last visit.

Tolstoy's last letter to his wife said "life is not a joke," echoing the last entry in Alexander Ivanov's notebooks, "It is not permissible to joke with God." Father Ambrose of Optyna's last words after seeing Tolstoy shortly before his death were "very proud" (*gord—ochen*).

Tolstoy's combination of pride and moral seriousness helped give modern Russian literature a distinctive cast. Writers henceforth seemed to be trying to say that, if morality could no longer be derived from the teachings of the Church, it had to be somehow rooted in nature itself. The answer to the facades of imperial Petersburg lay in the restorative beauty and ambient spaces of rural Russia. Tolstoy was laid to rest in 1910 in a small clearing within the forest on his country estate, Yasnaya Polyana (literally "clear glade"), with only a small green seedling as a gravestone.

Tolstoy had greater influence on Gandhi and modern India than on Russia, but he played an enormous role in delegitimizing Tsarist authority. As the barefoot sage on his wooded estate near Tula just south of Moscow, he became in many ways the conscience of Russia even if he never became its leader. Visits to Tolstoy became the moral alternative to audiences with the Tsar. Tolstoy's rejection of modern industrialism as well as traditional authority made him the symbolic alternative to autocracy: a kind of secular saint for the new cultural elite, the independent intelligentsia that had replaced the state aristocracy as the dominant force in Russian culture by the late 19th century.

The literature of an intellectual elite, however, could

not reach the emotions of the illiterate peasant population that had begun to stream into Petersburg in the last years of Gogol's life. Russian artists faced the challenge of finding some new means of communicating with ordinary people. Both architecture and painting seemed to have failed to connect with the masses and to have exhausted themselves with pretentious projects that stifled creativity.

But a new medium of expression was emerging which spoke directly to the emotions and had not yet been seriously developed in Russia. Gogol seems to have seen it coming. As he gradually abstracted himself from the material world in his late years, the bells on his troika seemed to get louder and louder. As more and more Russians were beginning to experience a measure of freedom, they began to discover the most immaterial—yet emotional and conducive to action—of all the art forms: music. In an unpublished fragment that he left behind at his death, Gogol wrote:

> Only in music does man have freedom. Everywhere he is in fetters. He forges for himself even heavier fetters than those imposed on him by society and authority... He is free only when he loses himself in a frenzied dance: here his soul no longer fears his body.

Long after Gogol's troubled soul had left his body, this prophecy came back, like the ghost of Akaky Akakevich in his "Overcoat," to unnerve the centers of power. The frenzy of music and dance that swept through Russia in the late 19th and early 20th centuries represented a delayed explosion of this unfettered freedom. At the same time, this sudden profusion of music enabled Russians to continue through yet another medium of expression Gogol's and Ivanov's quest for the renewal of Russia through art.

PART III

THE MASSES

Defeat in war ended the silence of the Russian countryside. In the Crimean War of 1853–56, Russia was beaten on its own soil for the first time in 150 years. Without railroads south of Moscow, the mighty Nicholas I had been unable to move his troops to the distant Crimea in time to defeat England and France, who had allied themselves with the Muslim Turks and shattered the myth that the Russian Empire was invincible. Gone forever was the fantasy (reinforced by the defeat of the revolutions of 1848–49 in Europe) that the "Holy Alliance" of Orthodox Russia, Protestant Prussia, and Catholic Austria was a modern Holy Trinity of Kingdoms that could protect Christian civilization from infidel Islam on the one side and Anglo-French liberalism on the other.

When the new Tsar, Alexander II, ascended to the throne in 1855, he opened up Russia to radical change based on Western ideas. This pattern of a lost war precipitating change was to be repeated with ever more revolutionary consequences after Russia was defeated by Japan in 1904–05, and beaten into exhaustion by the Germans in 1914–18.

The authority of the landed nobility was shaken not merely because its aristocratic officer class had been defeated in war, but also because Western liberal ideas were undermining the aristocracy's very reason for existence. Alexander II, in the early 1860s, undercut aristocratic power in the countryside by—in rapid succession—freeing the serfs, creating a new form of local government (the *zemstvos*), and introducing a new system of trial by jury. The aristocracy lost some of its traditional rural power base once slaves no longer did the work and non-aristocrats at the local level acquired a role in both exercising power and dispensing justice.

During the reign of Alexander II, prose literature cascaded forth as never before or since in Russian history. Its stock characters, the "superfluous man" and the "repenting nobleman," dramatized the aristocrats' sense of their own growing irrelevance to the developing life of the country they lived in. Writers did not, for the most part, find positive heroes in the aristocracy. Nor—surprisingly enough—did they often depict the tribulations of individual people in ways that could elicit sympathy for them as Gogol had done. Instead, Russian writers became fixated during this period on idealizing "the people" as a collective force for transforming Russia and inspiring a morality that they no longer found in religion.

The rising masses that the fading aristocracy was discovering had no faces, not even names with patronymics that identified their fathers. The people were part of the landscape rather than the population. They were addressed by patronizingly familiar nicknames such as children give their toys. There was not even an agreed collective designation for this rising force. Practical people in the cities talked in a matter-of-fact way about *liudi*, derived from the German word for "people" (*Leute*). Urban intellectuals still talked about them as "peasants" derived from the Russian words for both "cross" and "Christians" (*krestiane—krest—khristiane*), even if they had moved to the cities. The playwright Alexander Ostrovsky used the Gogolian term *glush'* or "remote place"; the poet Alexander Blok, the word *tma*, meaning simply "darkness"; and the filmmaker Sergei Eisenstein, the word "caviar"—suggesting that, though its tiny parts had no individuality, the congealed mass itself was the ultimate delicacy for the gourmet palate.

When literary aristocrats discovered the new phenomenon of the masses amidst the upheavals of the 1860s, they described it simply as *narod*—a word that was as vague in meaning as it was rich in suggestion. It was derived from the word *rod*, meaning family, heredity, and generation—the very phenomena that had legitimized the aristocracy's authority. These qualities were now being invested in the people as a whole with a word that both looked back to its meaning of "nation" in Nicholas I's doctrine of official nationalism and forward to the revolutionary notion of "the people" as a collective source of social justice and moral regeneration.

But the everyday life of the masses was being transformed by metal and machines. Suddenly, under Alexander II, the wooden world of rural Muscovy and the stone and stucco world of aristocratic Petersburg were being invaded everywhere by the metallic might of a new industrial culture. The sound of steam engines was beginning to drown out the bells on Gogol's troika, and the noise was popularly seen as a dangerous, perhaps satanic foreign intrusion.

The Old Believers had opposed the introduction of clocks in the 17th century because they substituted metallic machines that measured time mechanically for the natural rhythms of the seasons and the church calendar. They saw the placing of a large English clock on the Kremlin walls as a sign of the coming of the Antichrist. In like manner, the spread of rail lines was now seen as the appearance of Star Wormwood from the Book of Revelation. The very word for train station (*vokzal*) was taken from the English place name Vauxhall: the first stop out of London which Russians discovered when they went to England and visited the famed Crystal Palace, the central building created for the great Victorian Exposition of 1851. Dostoevsky saw in this gigantic metal and glass emporium of secular progress an apocalyptical threat to a Russia still living close to nature and traditional religious faith.

But metal was on the march; and the masses were riding the "iron road" (the literal meaning of the Russian word for railroad) into cities increasingly preoccupied with metal and machines. For the first time in history, iron supports had been built into a dome, the largest dome in Petersburg, St. Isaac's Cathedral. Iron bridges proliferated, and many of the factories that grew up around the aristocratic core of the city were either made of iron or filled with metal machinery. Steam engines were soon joined by turbines for an expanding fleet and then by internal combustion engines for automotive transportation. Most important of all was the continuous growth in the metallic weapons of an expanding army which—for the first time in the 1870s—was fueled by universal conscription.

The peculiarly hard political machine that the Russian revolutionary movement eventually produced bore the mark of metal from the beginning. The very first revolutionary circle that Lenin organized was in the St. Petersburg Imperial Technological Institute. It lay on the outskirts rather than in the imperial center of the city. Its building was centered not on the traditional chapel or lecture hall, but on the giant dynamo that the

Siemens Company had planted in the main atrium—
and on the student cafeteria, which the revolutionaries
regarded as Russia's first liberated zone, referring to it as
their *sich:* the name for the free zone on the lower
Dnieper River where the Zaporozhian Cossacks held
their councils. In the shadow of the machine and over
conversations in the cafeteria, Lenin formed his first circle and met his future wife and revolutionary companion, Nadezhda Krupskaia.

Joseph Dzhugashvili, the man who succeeded Lenin
and imposed the cruelest form of forced industrialization
on the Russian people, took his revolutionary name,
Stalin, from the Russian word for steel. Symbolic of the
cruelty with which Stalin's Communist Party machine
moved the Russian empire to metal in the 1930s was the
coerced construction of the totally new city of Magnitogorsk. It was built around a mountain of metal, rising like
a votive offering to the man of steel, seeming to draw
slave laborers to it the way a magnet (the literal meaning
of the *magnit* in Magnitogorsk) draws loose metal filings
to it. Unprecedented numbers were sent to their deaths
in order to extract gold and other precious metals from
the frozen wastes of the North.

The massive metal of Russian tanks and *katyusha* rockets did, however, help Russia defeat Nazi Germany in
World War II. This victory partly relegitimized a regime
that had lost all moral authority during the great purges
of the 1930s. And the thrust of metallic spaceships provided a continuing symbol of might and majesty that enabled the Russian empire to survive longer than that of
any other great European power. Metal was shredded into
medals, which were awarded in unprecedented numbers

to workers who showed by their own example "how the steel was tempered"—and were able to survive the industrial as well as the military "shock campaigns" of the Soviet era.

Russia's Iron Age was legitimized for the masses by the first machine-made art form: the cinema. Moving pictures created the myth of an all-liberating revolution and a host of heroes for Communist construction. But films also played a key role in delegitimizing Communism in the post-Stalin era. The new art form of the 20th century enabled Russia's humanistic culture of the 19th century to triumph in the end over the totalitarian Frankenstein monster it had inadvertently helped to create.

The ultimate impotence of metallic might against moral force was demonstrated in the final failure of the Communist Party machine to sustain itself by a massive tank invasion of Moscow in the coup attempt of August, 1991. This desperate attempt to hold on to power in a rapidly changing Russia was supported by the largest and most heavily metallic armed force ever assembled under one single political authority in human history. The 5.5 million people in uniform were defeated without a shot being fired by a small, largely unarmed gathering around the government center of Russia's first elected President, Boris Yeltsin.

Communism was repudiated not just because Russians had discovered new forms of human communication and the possibilities of freedom, but also because they were rediscovering their own deeper traditions of moral and religious responsibility.

Russians have historically attached special significance to events that fall on important days in the church calendar. The coup attempt began on the Feast of the Transfiguration just as the Patriarch was celebrating a liturgy in the Kremlin's Cathedral of the Assumption and opening the coronation doors for the first time since the Communist Revolution to address the people in the Kremlin Square.

Yeltsin's moral authority was solidified when he asked forgiveness from the parents of the three young men who died accidentally during the resistance to the coup. "Forgive me, your president, that I was unable to defend and save your sons." Someone who was not to blame was accepting responsibility in a society where everyone had avoided taking responsibility for anything. "Forgive me" is what many Russians say to whoever is nearest them before taking communion. "Forgive" is the last word uttered by the hero of Tchaikovsky's great historical opera *Mazepa* and by Boris Godunov in the greatest of all Russian national operas.

Communist machine rule was ritually repudiated the day after the coup collapsed by the giant rally which dismantled the largest of all metallic statues in Moscow: that of the founder of the Soviet secret police, Felix Dzerzhinsky. Russia was rediscovering its deeper self. The high point of the largest rally against the coup when the outcome was still in doubt was the speech in front of the Winter Palace by the greatest scholar of Old Russian culture and the last living representative of pre-revolutionary, humanistic Petersburg, Dmitry Likhachev.

On the second night of the stand-off, when a Communist attack on the Russian White House was generally expected, the Patriarch anathematized fraternal bloodshed by means of a public prayer for the Virgin's protection used during the fast in preparation for the Assumption. Russia's first post-Communist Parliament was formally opened at the end of the putsch crisis by a liturgy in the Cathedral of the Assumption on the Feast of the Assumption.

Chapter 4

The Sounds of the People: The Music of Musorgsky

It is particularly hard for Americans to understand that as late as the mid-19th century, Russian classical music virtually did not exist. After all, Russian music deeply and directly influenced American music as it rose to dominate the soundscape of the 20th century. When Carnegie Hall opened in New York in 1891, the great Russian composer Peter Tchaikovsky was invited to come over to inaugurate it. His 20th century successors—Rachmaninov, Prokofiev, Stravinsky—all spent much of their lives in America. When the symphony orchestras of Boston and Washington ascended to world renown, it was under the baton of Koussevitsky and Rostropovich. What Piatagorsky and Rostropovich did to make the cello popular in America, Chaliapin did for the bass voice, Nureyev and Baryshnikov did for the ballet, Balanchine did for choreography, and the list goes on.

Russia's first democratically elected President reminded democratic America that its most beloved patriotic anthem of the 20th century was written by an emigrant from Russia, born in the Siberian city of Tiumen. Boris Yeltsin ended his speech to a Joint Session of Congress in June, 1992, by saying "In the words of that great American of Russian origin, Irving Berlin, 'God Bless America'— and, I would add, Russia too."

How can so much music have come so fast from a culture in which the very idea of "playing" music had historically been viewed as a kind of blasphemy, if not temptation of the devil? The very word for music in Russian is derived from Polish. There were no Western-style musical notes used or instruments permitted in Russian Orthodox churches. Nothing was to compete with the austere majesty of the liturgy, which was sung in unaccompanied plainsong and framed by the ringing of bells to radiate sanctity out to the community before and after a service.

Russian minstrels or *Skomorokhi* were repeatedly persecuted and their instruments burned in 17th-century Moscow. The modest musical accompaniment to the court culture of 18th-century Petersburg was largely produced by foreigners and confined to small theatres for aristocratic audiences. There was no organ music in the soul and very little instrumental music in the body of old Russia. Silence had been the ultimate ideal of monastic Russia; and, as prisoners were sent off in the 19th century into the endless silence of Siberia, even their song of lamentation represented a semi-masochistic embrace of the silence that had been forced upon them.

> No sound from the city is heard
> Over the Nevsky Tower is silence.
> And on the bayonets of our guards
> Glistens the midnight moon.

Even in the early 19th century, pioneering Russian composers worked mainly abroad. Censors at the border confiscated the scores of the 20-year-old composer and virtuoso pianist Anton Rubinstein when he returned to Russia in 1849—apparently fearing that musical notation was some kind of secret revolutionary code.

At a deeper level than he could have ever understood, the ignorant censor may have sensed what was coming, because the sudden, dramatic explosion of Russian music that occurred in the late 19th and early 20th centuries coincided with—and can help us understand—the concurrent rise of the Russian revolutionary movement.

Music found both its distinctive national voice and its first mass audience in Russia through the manic efforts of five largely untrained composers. They overturned previous musical as well as social conventions in order to give expression to the deepest longings of the forgotten, suffering, ordinary people of Russia.

Modest Musorgsky was the genius of this group, which was called in the rough, populist language of the time "the mighty heap." Musorgsky's very name contained the word for "trash" (*musor*); and he explained that it was his task " to plow up the black earth . . . the virgin soil . . . that no man has touched . . . to penetrate unexplored regions and conquer them . . . moving past all the shadows, *to unknown shores.*"

Russia's sudden plunge into music in the 1860s illustrates particularly well the pattern we have already noted in the Russian discovery of a new art form: first, the wholesale initial adoption of a finished foreign model; second, the creation of a totally original Russian variant, which, at the same time, overloads the art form with ex-

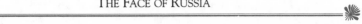
pectations that it can somehow transform Russia; and third and last, the sudden breakdown and breakup of the art form—and its subsequent replacement by yet another medium of art, which becomes the next vehicle for expressing the aspirations of an age as well as the enduring Russian quest to find salvation rather than just entertainment in art.

The finished foreign model was European grand opera, which dazzled Petersburg in the season of 1862–63 first with the world premiere of Verdi's *Force of Destiny* commissioned by Tsar Alexander II and then with the appearance of Richard Wagner as guest conductor. The creation of an original Russian variant followed the corporate decision of the "mighty heap" in that very season to bypass the Petersburg Conservatory altogether and create a new kind of "people's music drama" that was exemplified by Musorgsky's *Boris Godunov*. The metaphysical overload came with Musorgsky's effort to compose an even more ambitious encore: *Khovanshchina*, which he never completed—and which, in any case, like Gogol's *Dead Souls*, represented only part of an unfinished trilogy.

The basic subject matter for Russian opera was Russian history and Russian folklore—the source of inspiration respectively for *A Life for the Tsar* (1836) and *Ruslan and Lyudmila* (1842), the two path-breaking operas by the "father of Russian music," Mikhail Glinka. But it was not until the relaxation of stage censorship under Alexander II in the 1860s that a large amount of distinctively Russian opera burst onto the stage. The German musical world was impressed by Rubinstein's 13 operas and four "spiritual operas" (oratorios) and by the majestic staging and orchestral richness of three major operas by the great music critic, Alexander Serov (*Judith*, 1863, *Rogneda*, 1865, and *The Power of Evil*, 1871). But these important works were increasingly dismissed (and have been unfairly neglected ever since) as being too imitative of the West. Russians soon developed an intense special attachment to the more original works of Musorgsky and his friends.

The golden age of Russian national opera began in 1868 when Musorgsky finished the first draft of *Boris Godunov*. It continued until Borodin and Tchaikovsky died in the early 1890s and Nicholas Rimsky-Korsakov, the last and most prolific of the original "mighty heap," finished his last opera, *The Golden Cockerel*, in 1907.

The composition of operas broke down in Russia almost as dramatically as it had broken out 40 years earlier. But the breakup was itself immensely creative—involving the dissonant, Dionysian leap into modernism of Stravinsky's *Rite of Spring*, the megalomanic *Mysterium* of Scriabin in which colors and smells were orchestrated along with sounds, and the *Persimfans* in the early Communist regime: the world's first orchestra without a conductor, whose role was abolished as a tyrannical holdover from the authoritarian past.

So rich and variegated were the sounds of music during Russia's revolutionary agony of the early 20th century that the greatest poet of the age, Alexander Blok, suggested in the title of a famous essay that the revolution itself was an expression of "the spirit of music." In his famous poem, "The Twelve," Blok likened a revolutionary group entering Petersburg to the apostles following Christ, and cheered them on with lines that were themselves musical—simulating the sounds of the cold wind blowing through that coldest of cities:

Revoliutsionny derzhiti shag.
Neugamonny ne dremlit vrag.

(Keep the revolutionary pace.
The enemy is unforgiving.)

How did this explosion of music, which was almost entirely the work of apolitical, conservative Russians, unwittingly help set the stage for revolution? Basically it did so by engaging the emotions subliminally in a way no other media can, and by investing a kind of secular divinity in the Russian people. Their oral traditions and spontaneous improvisations were thought to be the source and subject matter for a new kind of music. The new composers still clung to the old tradition of the sung liturgy—that music should be linked to words that carry a message—but they were determined that their music would both exemplify and benefit the poorer classes and not merely instruct and impress them.

When Alexander II liberated the serfs, he opened up the possibility of broader participation in what had been a highly elitist culture. For a still largely illiterate people, music was a particularly effective means of communication, and it rapidly moved onto a stage that had been set for it by the previous accomplishments of Russian culture.

The 18th-century Russian aristocracy had sought to contain its stratified society within what Goethe later called "the frozen music" of architecture. Monumental buildings, heroic statuary, court rituals, and military parades had made Petersburg itself into an intimidating open-air theatre of empire. But the growing strength within the city of both nonaristocratic professional people and a transplanted peasant work force led art beyond words into more accessible audio-visual media. Aristocratic architecture was melting into music for the masses.

The sense that they were creating a distinctively new Russian music convinced Musorgsky and his friends that they should work altogether apart from the newly founded St. Petersburg Conservatory (Russia's first) in the turbulent winter of 1862–63. They were not only breaking away from the perceived westernizing bias of the official culture which had welcomed both Verdi and Wagner to St. Petersburg. They were also participating in the unprecedented wave of student protest movements that shut down St. Petersburg University, rocked all of Russia in the wake of peasant emancipation, and inspired radical young painters to leave the Academy of Arts during the same year.

Young painters were rebelling against the Germanic mythological subject prescribed for their annual highly traditional and conservative competition: "The Entry of Wotan into Valhalla." They called themselves "wanderers" (*peredvizhniki*) and set out realistically to depict the simple people and places of their native land. Young composers followed suit.

Their secret, common hope was to find in the ordinary *muzhik* the warmth and wisdom they had not found in Petersburg. The painters and musicians wanted to lose themselves in the people in order to help realize freedom for the people. The very phrase "freedom of the people" was musical, *svoboda naroda*, and became almost

a ritual incantation in the political poetry of this reformist period.

Musorgsky had been fascinated by Russian folksongs
during his childhood on an estate in the Pskov region; he
arranged dozens of them for piano and voice after leaving
a promising military career at age 19 to devote himself
entirely to music. Musorgsky was also drawn to the stage.
With typical Russian megalomania he immediately
turned in 1859 to providing music for perhaps the two
greatest tragic dramas of all time: Sophocles' *Oedipus Rex*
and Shakespeare's *King Lear*. He sought to write a choral
version of the former and to provide an overture and in-
termezzo for the work his mentor Mily Balakirev was writing on the latter. Four years later he began to compose a
choral work, *King Saul*, and his first opera, *Salambo*, a
drama of ancient Carthage based on a novel by Flaubert.

None of these works was ever finished, but parts of
them reappear in later compositions. The praying chorus
of *Oedipus* recurs in the music of slave revolt in *Salambo*
and in the battle scene in *Mlada*, an unusual mix of opera
and ballet that was commissioned collectively for the entire "mighty heap," but completed by Rimsky-Korsakov.
The battle chorus in *Salambo* is folded into a later choral
work, *Jesus Navin* (1877). All four of his subsequent operas also use elements recycled from earlier works. Three
of them were never completed.

Musorgsky's entire corpus of musical composition can
be seen as a continuing chronicle of expressive themes
with many variations. He never assigned opus numbers to
his works and argued that music itself does not follow
fixed laws, but is rather an evolving activity that "pro-
gresses like the spiritual life of man." He saw his art not

as an end in itself, but as "a means of conversation with the people."

Musorgsky wedded his love of Russia with his thirst for tragic drama on a grand scale in *Boris Godunov,* the one opera he did complete—and, in fact, re-completed in a second version as well. He was led to this subject by his passionate desire, typical of the period, to unearth the true language of the Russian people and to present it in a dramatic musical form that would both liberate and unite the Russian people.

In search of the secret, inner cadences of Russian speech, the "mighty heap" turned to the still new world of Russian literature for the texts in which to find both the inner music and the deeper message that would bring deliverance to the Russian people. The pioneer of the group, Alexander Dargomyzhsky, started it all with his last opera, *The Stone Guest,* which has been called "the most influential total failure in all musical history." He took for his text Pushkin's poetic retelling of the same story that Mozart had used in *Don Giovanni,* but sought to derive the music entirely from the inflection of Pushkin's words. The idea was born that opera should be a continuous recitative based on a seamless series of short, irregular phrases. The orchestra was to be subordinated to the voice, and arias eliminated altogether.

This original idea inspired Musorgsky suddenly to change his musical course and to derive his own music from a Russian literary text. In order to go deeper into the "black earth" of ordinary life he turned to Gogol rather than Pushkin. He sought to translate into music the essence of prose rather than the letter of poetry. In a two-week fever of excited inspiration he transformed one of

Gogol's short stories into the famed four-part orchestral suite *St. John's Night on Bald Mountain*. In contrast to his usual practice of composing only the piano score, Musorgsky wrote out the full orchestration—staying awake the entire night of Midsummer (St. John's) to complete it.

Musorgsky next turned, at Dargomyzhsky's suggestion, to deriving an opera from Gogol's play *The Marriage*, and in so doing—as he put it—"crossed the Rubicon" into a genuinely new type of operatic idiom. Though he loved Gogol's depiction of rural life and would return later for another attempt at an opera based on a Gogol text, *The Sorochinsky Fair*, Musorgsky finished only one act of *The Marriage*—finding that the comic subject "contains too little of big-hearted Mother Russia."

Musorgsky and his colleagues took Glinka's dual fascination with history and folklore as the starting point for their efforts to find the true music of "big-hearted Mother Russia." Mily Balakirev, the ideological leader of the "heap," gave Russian opera a new international notoriety in 1867 when he dazzled the musical world of the Hapsburgs with his energetic conducting of both of Glinka's operas back-to-back in Prague. He returned in triumph to Russia to work with the group to create the Russian answer to Verdi and Wagner.

All the Russians had begun as imitators of the West. Musorgsky and Borodin first met in 1856 at an evening when Musorgsky played the piano and sang selections from *Traviata* and *Trovatore*. And Musorgsky's first attempt to write an opera in that same year followed Verdi in trying to adopt a Victor Hugo text (*Han d'Islande*).

Their group was, however, determined to make music broadly available to the Russian masses. This was the avowed purpose of the Russian Musical Society, created in 1858. They also participated in the Sunday School movement, through which aristocratic students volunteered to teach peasants and workers on Sunday some of the things they themselves were learning in classes during the week. They began meeting regularly on Saturday evenings during 1860–61 in the home of Balakirev.

Balakirev had a special aura: an enormous beard, smiling eyes, and a youth spent in the deep interior of Russia in relative poverty. He wrote an overture *Rus* in 1862 for the millennium of the establishment of the first Russian government (the legendary summoning of Rurik to Novgorod). And he had been close to Glinka before he left Russia in 1856 to die abroad the following year. Pushkin had passed his mantle to Gogol in literature. Glinka seemed to have done the same to Balakirev for music. And Balakirev, in turn, was Musorgsky's first mentor, introducing him to Glinka's sister, who became a kind of mother figure to Musorgsky. Balakirev worked with Musorgsky on his earliest compositions in 1859 and conducted the first public performance of a completed choral work by Musorgsky, *The Destruction of Sennacherib*, in January, 1867.

Balakirev had made an extensive visit back to his native Volga region in 1860 to gather folksongs, the replaying and reshaping of which soon became a major feature of the meetings of the group. Musorgsky was to spend time in Balakirev's home town of Nizhni Novgorod trying to listen to the natural sounds of people as they came from all over the Russian heartland to the annual fair in that ancient city.

Balakirev's circle was first called "the mighty heap" in

a review of the free concert of all-Slavic music that Balakirev conducted in Petersburg on his return from Prague
in 1867. It was a typical commune of the period: an expression of the generational rebellion described in Turgenev's classic novella *Fathers and Sons* (1861). The
youthful hero of that work rejects not just traditional pa-
ternal authority, but the impractical idealism of the
landed gentry. He sees no value in inherited ideas or practices and describes himself as a "nihilist" who believes
only in the scientific method: "Two plus two equals four
and all the rest is nonsense."

Musorgsky's musical commune sought not just to celebrate their own freedom from tradition, but also to connect with "big-hearted Mother Russia." In a time of continuing social upheaval they were attracted by that most
social of the arts: the stage. Living in a period of historic
change, they were irresistibly drawn for subject matter—
as Glinka had been even in more tranquil times—to Russia's original "Time of Troubles" in the late 16th and early
17th centuries. This was a period of interregnum, when
the old political legitimacy (the hereditary royal succession that ended with Ivan the Terrible) had broken down,
no new one had been established, and chaos, conflict,
and poverty reigned in Russia.

Russia in the 1860s was descending into a new, revolutionary "Time of Troubles." Seeking to find "the present
in the past," Musorgsky turned to the subject of Boris Godunov, who had the misfortune to rule from 1598 to 1605
as Russia's first non-hereditary ruler. The first of a series of
assassination attempts by revolutionaries against Alexander II occurred in 1866. A mounting crescendo of murders of Tsarist officials during the next 15 years culmi-

nated in the assassination of Tsar Alexander in March, 1881, two weeks before Musorgsky died—like Gogol—at night and at the age of 42.

This revolutionary campaign was the work of young intellectuals, who eventually coalesced into a group called "The People's Will." This was the first organization in human history to adopt the word "terrorism" as a badge of pride. By substituting bombs for rifle shots, they truly did terrorize the entire population, providing a new kind of drama for the open air theatre that was St. Petersburg. The selfless sincerity of the terrorists seriously unnerved the imperial establishment. Juries often acquitted the killers—moved by their impassioned defense of their cause and by the fact that many were women and some even pregnant. When the Tsar lay dying from one terrorist's bomb, another propped up his head with the reserve bomb so that the Tsar could take a final drink of water.

But the revolution did not materialize, and the imperial parade continued. This was, in fact, the golden age of the Russian marching band. Brass instruments in the open air for a conscript army replaced the quieter strings and woodwinds of earlier, more narrowly aristocratic ensembles. Band music both mobilized and disciplined emotions on the broad boulevards of Petersburg. The Russian national anthem of 1833 had been plagiarized from a Prussian military march. The man who best orchestrated the chaotic sounds of the "mighty heap" was Russia's inspector of Naval Orchestras, Nicholas Rimsky-Korsakov.

Rimsky composed his First Symphony in 1865, and conducted a kind of running seminar on instrumental music for the "heap." Balakirev wrote three symphonies in the 1860s. One was entitled *Rus*; another attempted to transpose the bubbling sounds of conversation in a railroad station. Balakirev worked for a time as a porter in order to "listen" to the natural rhythms of speech used by those coming into Petersburg from the countryside. Dargomyzhsky died in January, 1869, on the very night he listened to the first performance of Borodin's first symphony, which was thought to be ushering in a new and distinctively Russian symphonic idiom.

But it was in opera that the group most fully and collectively expressed itself. Borodin gave epic exuberance, even Tolstoyan dimensions, to his one opera, *Prince Igor*. Musorgsky brought psychological drama, even Dostoevskian depth, to his one completed opera, *Boris Godonov*. Rimsky-Korsakov was involved from beginning to end—from his pathfinding work *Maid of Pskov* in 1868 until his death in 1908.

Rimsky's subject in his *Maid of Pskov* was Ivan the Terrible and the onset of Russia's original "Time of Troubles." It was an intensely political subject. Sergei Solovev's 29-volume *History of Russia*, the most exhaustive ever written, had devoted its entire sixth volume to promoting a relatively favorable view of Ivan. A spate of plays contested that view; and the censors were conducting a running war with the playwrights. Tchaikovsky wrote a conventionally melodramatic opera about Ivan, *Oprichniki*, but Rimsky wrote a very different work: the first Russian opera in which the chorus dominates the action and nostalgia is evident for the communal political institutions of the medieval past.

The relatively free city of Pskov is the real hero of the opera, and the ringing of the bell for its assembly (the so-called *veche*) echoes throughout. Rimsky gives the opera a politically correct happy ending, as the crowd in Pskov welcomes Ivan the Terrible, who will silence the bell of independence and centralize all power in Moscow. But the greatest impact—both dramatically and musically—is made by depicting on stage what one critic described as "a real Russian people's assembly."

Rimsky returned to the reign of Ivan much later with his more purely lyrical *The Tsar's Bride* as well as a one-act opera to precede the *Maid of Pskov* and plans for yet another opera that would continue the story. Rimsky never completed his own trilogy. But he did complete the orchestration for Musorgsky's uncompleted operatic trilogy: *Boris*, which dealt with the "Time of Troubles" that followed Ivan's death, and *Khovanshchina*, which depicted the chaos that preceded Peter the Great. Rimsky was Musorgsky's closest musical collaborator, and *Boris* in many ways flows directly out of the *Maid of Pskov*. Rimsky not only made Russian music more harmonically acceptable, he also served as the bridge over which Russian music passed from reactionary militarism to revolutionary modernism.

The new Russian composers worked in a communal way like the icon painters of old—and like the revolutionary circles of the same era. Most of the work was done by people who had other jobs and gathered in evenings, on weekends, and above all during the long sunlit summers when they could work together in the countryside of the Russian North. An idea suggested by Balakirev would form the basis of a piano improvisation by Musorgsky, would be written down by Cui, dipped for preservation purposes into a chemical solution made by Borodin, one of the leading scientists of his day, and finally orchestrated by Rimsky-Korsakov, who linked the group with the one great Russian composer of the era who was not part of it, but was influenced by it, Peter Ilich Tchaikovsky.

There was an amazing similarity of subject matter used in the parallel careers of the great composers of Russian opera, Musorgsky, Tchaikovsky, and Rimsky. The first flush of operatic creativity for each in the late 1860s and early 1870s began with an historical opera on the "Time of Troubles." Then each turned from history to folklore—composing an opera on a story of Gogol's: Musorgsky's *Sorochinsky Fair*, Tchaikovsky's *Slippers* and Rimsky's *May Night*. Finally, Musorgsky and Tchaikovsky both turned back to history—to the period that ended the breakup of Old Russia and brought revolutionary change under Peter the Great: Musorgsky's *Khovanshchina* and Tchaikovsky's *Mazepa*—in many ways their most magnificent yet most mournful works.

Boris Godunov was and remains the perfect example of the new kind of "popular music drama" that the "mighty heap" idealized. The Russian people were the center of the drama, not Boris himself. He is guilty before the people from his first words at coronation ("My soul is heavy") to his last word before dying ("forgive"). Music was subordinate to a message as it had been in the church tradition. The dominant voices are those of the bass voice and the chorus, the secular equivalent of the priest and the congregation in liturgical worship. But the message was found not just in Pushkin's literary text, but also in the ordinary speech and inner feelings of people in the deep interior of Russia.

Musorgsky sought to depict in music the sounds of rural vitality that Gogol had described in *Sorochinsky Fair*, the title of another of his unfinished operas. But he personally went deeper into the interior, to the even larger fair at Nizhni Novgorod. This ancient city stood at the intersection of the Volga and Kama rivers (rather like St. Louis at the confluence of the Missouri and Mississippi rivers), and its historic fair was the annual meeting place for all manner of voices from the Russian provinces.

The painter Repin produced, after many sketches, his great image of *Haulers on the Volga* (see illustration 25). He and the other "wanderers" increasingly journeyed out to that *mat rodnaia*, the "native mother" of Russian rivers, to gain closer contact with the unspoiled Russian people. Musorgsky was convinced that he could find a positive message as well as hidden melody in the great babbling sounds of Russia conversing with itself at its greatest national fair.

The central problem of the age was where would Russia find guidance for its development now that Alexander II had let the genie of reform out of the authoritarian bottle. He had raised high hopes with his reforms in the early 1860s, but halted the program and reasserted strong autocratic controls in the later part of the decade. Russia now faced a classic "revolution of rising expectations."

Musorgsky explored the problem of where Russia was heading with brilliant, even prophetic insight in the final scene of *Boris Godunov*. A mob has gathered in the Kromy Forest after Boris has died. This is a totally original scene not present in Pushkin's play and written rapidly in a genuine burst of inspiration. It was called "the revolutionary scene," and was banned from public performances during the revolution of 1905. Whatever it suggests about the mood of the people in the original "Time of Troubles" in the early 17th century, it tells us a great deal about the answers being explored in the 1860s and 1870s for a new basis of authority in Russia, through a strange series of individuals who appear before the leaderless Russian people.

At the beginning, a nobleman is reviled by the mob, who give him a whip for a scepter and a 100-year-old peasant woman for a queen. He represents the hereditary aristocracy who had derived their authority from the Tsar and were now being mocked with the magnificent chorus: "Praise the nobleman, praise Boris," *Slava boyarynu, Slava Borisovu.* This chorus throbs through the scene and was sung by some of the radical students who heard it first in the spring of 1874 just before they set forth into the countryside on their famous "movement to the people" during the "mad summer" of that year. They sought to find *kromy* forests of their own as they fanned out in what proved to be a vain attempt to mobilize the peasantry for radical social reform.

The second alternative authority to appear before the people is the prophetic holy fool, who had earlier in the opera called Boris a "Tsar-Herod." This was an insult to royalty unprecedented on a Russian stage. It was later seen by many to be directed against Stalin when the role was played by Ivan Kozlovsky, the great Ukrainian tenor, who was thought to speak for that land, which had suffered so much under the dictator (see illustration 26).

The fool represented the longing for a pure Christ figure, so central to Dostoevsky's *Idiot* and his "Legend of the Grand Inquisitor" in *The Brothers Karamazov.* One of the most popular of the giant paintings of the era, Vasily

Surikov's *Boyaryna Morozova*, shows a holy fool in the foreground (see illustration 10). One of Musorgsky's most moving early songs, "Svetik Savishna" of 1866, was the song of an inspired fool. His fool-in-Christ in *Boris* (like the idealistic students who went out to be with the peasants in the summer of 1874) is humiliated by an ungrateful mob.

The next figures to appear before the people are two fake holy men whom we met earlier in the opera when they told us in a drunken way how they helped Ivan the Terrible conquer Kazan. They are calling now for outright, violent revolution and the murder of the Tsar. A swelling chorus culminates in women crying "*Smert!*" (Death).

This represents an uncanny anticipation of the revolutionary populism that formed after the failure of the "movement to the people" of 1874. Students and intellectuals turned to direct action against government officials, and women played a central part in the group that eventually assassinated the Tsar. Musorgsky's Boris invokes the name of the pioneering professional revolutionary organization "The People's Will," which committed the assassination, at the climax of his mad scene. He shrieks that not he, but "the will of the people," caused the death of the young Dmitry.

Just at the climax of revolutionary excitement in the Kromy Forest scene, two Polish Jesuits arrive chanting Latin prayers in high tenor notes that Musorgsky contrasts with the deep bass voices of authentic Russians. The fake holy men incite the mob to drag off these ill-timed advocates of an unwanted Western alternative. They were arriving on the scene—as did the proposals for a Western-type constitution in Alexander II's last days—at a moment when revolutionary passions were aroused and the fate of alien moderation foredoomed.

The final force to come before the rebellious people is the Polish-sponsored False Dmitry himself, whom the gullible mob hails as the new Tsar. The vaunted Russian people thus end up no better off than they were at the beginning of the opera when we first meet them imploring Boris to become Tsar. They are simply trailing off behind a new Tsar who we know will be worse than the one he replaced. This is exactly what happened when the reactionary Alexander III succeeded the assassinated Alexander II.

The holy fool concludes the opera on an empty stage with a lacerating final lament about the coming of "dark, impenetrable darkness" in which there is nothing for a hungry people to do but weep. Having overturned the black earth of Russia, Musorgsky finds nothing but blackness, which becomes even more cosmic in the unfinished final opera that followed, *Khovanshchina*. It portrays the final days of Old Russia before the reforms of Peter the Great—an orgy of murders, divinations, and drinking that ends with a spectacular immolation scene in which an Old Believer priest leads everyone left on stage into a giant funeral pyre in the forest.

With Musorgsky, as with the greatest writers and painters of the age, a determination to tell the remorseless truth made it impossible to sustain the illusion that a message of deliverance could be found in the Russian masses. The new "people's music drama" of Russia had ultimately found sorrow in the nature of things, not hope in the ideals of people.

He might have completed *Khovanshchina* had he not expended so much time and energy in the 1870s on his two great but gloomy song cycles, *Without the Sun* and *Songs and Dances of Death*. At the end, he was writing only piano music as he spiraled down to death just a few days after Repin painted a haunting last portrait that served as a kind of icon for later composers (see illustration 27).

Well before he turned to writing *Boris Godunov*, Musorgsky had been preoccupied with the theme of the overthrow of kings (Oedipus, Lear, Sennacherib, Saul). None of the contending factions for power in *Khovanshchina* offers any hope for the suffering Russian people—least of all the reformist Peter the Great, whose shrilly trumpeted arrival at the end precipitates their tragic, final self-immolation.

There is no reason to believe that there would have been a happy ending had Musorgsky lived to write *Pugachevshchina*, the projected third part of what would have been a trilogy of operas on the people's suffering in Old Russia. This work, for which he gathered folk material intensively in 1877, was apparently to have been, like *Khovanshchina*, shaped by an original libretto and score that Musorgsky planned to write on the basis of direct immersion in primary materials. The tale of a popular rebel who led a major uprising against Catherine the Great partly in the name of the Old Believers ended with the grisly public dismembering of the leader, Pugachev, in Red Square. The story was at once full of too much exaggerated hope and too much final despair for Musorgsky's failing energies to tackle.

Musorgsky had a deeply unhappy personal life. He suf-

fered from nervous disorders and alcoholism from a rela-
tively early age; he never married, was subject to severe
depression, and may well have had fantasies that were
both erotic and violent. He left behind only a little more
than half of yet another ambitious artistic trilogy.

In many ways, his greatest legacy is his rich store of
rarely performed songs. They capture moods of nostalgia
and sadness as well as any of the great song cycles of the
19th century. He was a master at transcribing the sounds
of Russia into music—from the wind blowing in the park
at Tsarskoe Selo to the staccato of serial cannon fire. He
did not need words to describe people looking at "Pictures
from an Exhibition," or dawn by the Moscow River (in
the great prelude to *Khovanshchina*), or a monk writing a
chronicle (at the beginning of the scene in the monk's
cell in *Boris*).

Musorgsky saw himself as composing music for a kind
of ongoing chronicle of Russian culture. Whenever he
began to bring the elements of a composition together, he
would put a small Orthodox cross at the head of the
manuscript. And at the end, he gave the precise place
and date (often even the time of day) in the manner of a
monastic chronicler. Musorgsky approached the writing
of music as an act that could be justified only in service to
a higher calling. In the last analysis, he wrote, "we do not
need music, words, palette or chisel," but only "live
thoughts and direct conversation with the people."

The conversation that he conducted with "the people"
was reactionary in the deepest, monastic meaning of the
word. He was reacting to what he called "the horrifying
shark called civilization" that he saw destroying Russia
with the Western values of "easy gain...easy compos-

ing...and mild depravity." His metaphors run amok as he
likens Russia to "a large raft filled with the survivors of an
oceanic shipwreck." The Russian nation no longer hears
"those sounds which, like the remembrances of a mother
or dear friends, must make all living strings of a human
being vibrate." Russia must be rudely awakened to realize
both its own uniqueness and "the destructive oppression
that it is being subjected to." But the would-be doctors
are as dangerous as the disease. Russia is becoming

> a corpse, and the best people of this nation are [noth-
> ing more than] doctors who use electrogalvanic cur-
> rent to force the extremities of the corpse to jerk un-
> til it chemically disintegrates altogether.

Musorgsky anticipates the existential hopelessness of
much 20th-century art. Yet he imparted to Russian music
a passion for honesty and a sense of mission that helped
enable it to survive the galvanic shock of Stalinism. He
also passed on to posterity the sense that finding a distinctive voice for the Russian people was a continuing
corporate responsibility of Russian artists. The one piece
of music that he wrote specifically to defend his colleagues in "the mighty heap" took the form of a satire, but
had as its epigraph the Orthodox version of the words
pronounced just after the consecration of the elements of
communion: "All things come of thee, O Lord; and of
thine own have we given thee."

Russian opera in its brief golden age had taken Russian
culture once again through the familiar roller coaster of
borrowing, then transforming and finally exhausting another imported art form: in this case Verdian opera. Mu-

sorgsky had explored conventional Italian-type opera in his first unfinished opera, *Salambo*, which later provided some of the more lyrical passages for both *Boris* and *Khovanshchina*. One can trace the originality of Russian opera by describing four ways in which Musorgsky transformed into a Russian form the conventions Verdi had used to convey his revolutionary message.

Verdi had made the chorus the basic bearer of a collective call for the national liberation of the Italian people from Hapsburg rule. The great chorus of the Hebrews in bondage to Babylon in *Nabucco* (1842) was followed the next year by another powerful chorus of Christian crusaders seeking to liberate Jerusalem in *I Lombardi*. In many of his early operas, Verdi also introduced what might be called the Madonna-soprano, a feminine symbol of spiritual beauty often identified with the higher national ideal even more than with romance. The declamatory invocation to action in a Verdi opera was assigned to the tenor voice; and the great revolutionary Giuseppe Garibaldi, who had roomed with Lorenzo Salvi, an Italian tenor, in Staten Island, often seemed to be imitating the entries, exits, and declamations of a Verdian tenor during the Revolution of 1848. Finally, in his operas just during and after the Revolution of 1848, Verdi increasingly calls for revolution—culminating in a full-scale, onstage uprising in his *I Vespri Siciliani*.

Musorgsky transformed all of these conventions. As befits a culture edging toward social rather than national revolution, Musorgsky's chorus conveyed a message not of national hope but of popular suffering. Instead of suggesting salvation with a pure soprano, women are given minor importance in Musorgsky's operas—invited in as contraltos bearing exceptionally ill tidings like the icy Marina Mnishek in *Boris* or the eerie Martha in *Khovan-shchina*. And, as we have seen in the Kromy Forest scene, the declamatory moment of truth in Russian operas generally takes the form of a lament rather than a call to arms; the on-stage revolution leads not to liberation, but to renewed tyranny.

Russian opera was to have other glorious moments after the deaths of Musorgsky and Alexander II in March 1881. Tchaikovsky followed up his melodic *Eugene Onegin* (1879) with two other operas based on works by Pushkin that added new elements of psychological intensity (*Mazepa* of 1884 and *The Queen of Spades* in 1890). A new strain of pure Italian lyricism was superimposed on Russian subject matter in the 1890s—in the scene where Borodin's Prince Igor in Tatar captivity sighs for freedom and his wife, and in the lush mad scene at the end of Rimsky-Korsakov's *Tsar's Bride*.

The main energy of the musical stage, however, moved towards ballet in the 1880s and 1890s. The fairy tale lyricism and ethereal beauty of Tchaikovsky's *Swan Lake, Sleeping Beauty,* and *Nutcracker* compensated for the ugliness of life in the age of industrialization—just as the greatest icons had helped compensate for the brutalization of life under the Mongols.

Perhaps the truest heir to the Musorgskian tradition of people's music drama (based on recitative and on the perceived sounds of vernacular speech) was another Slav, the Czech Leos Janacek. He too went to the fair in Nizhni Novgorod in the 1890s in order to extract music from spontaneous Russian speech. He returned to found the Russian Circle in Moravia, which he idealized as the non-westernized part of his country the way the Russians came to prefer Moscow to Petersburg. Musorgsky had called Moscow Jericho, the Israelites' point of entry into the Promised Land, from the first time he visited it in 1859 and pronounced himself "transported into another world...close to everything Russian."

Janacek's last opera, *From the House of the Dead*, presses the Russian formula to its limits. It is a kind of extended tone poem—pure recitative without a single aria, unremittingly gloomy, and based on a great Russian literary text. It is the most impressive effort ever made to produce an opera from the most unmusical yet powerful of all the great Russian writers, Musorgsky's contemporary, Fedor Dostoevsky.

Of all the great Russian artists of the 19th century, Dostoevsky speaks the most eloquently to the 20th. He was very different from most Russian writers of his own time—belonging neither to the privileged aristocracy nor to the alienated intelligentsia, writing to earn a living with his wife by his side, basing his novels on stories in the newspapers, publishing his own stories serially in popular journals, and stripping away all depiction of nature and history in order to probe deeply into the psychological dramas taking place within man himself.

He had been active in the first circle of Russian utopian socialists on the eve of the revolutions of 1848, served a long sentence in a Siberian prison, and was converted there to Christianity by the simple faith of fellow prisoners. Behind the new radicalism that he encountered on his return from Siberia he saw the coming of a new type of "underground man" freed from all traditional moral restraints (*Notes from the Underground*, 1864) to commit murder for philosophical reasons (*Crime and Punishment*, 1864) or for political mobilization (*The Possessed*, 1871–72).

Dostoevsky's dramatic plots are woven out of the depth of people's interdependence and of the schisms that exist within society, in the closest human relationships, and within individuals. He introduced into Russian literature a hero with a split personality in his short novel of 1846, *The Double*. He wrote the term for schism (*raskol*) into the very name of Raskolnikov, the central figure of *Crime and Punishment*; and he built his final masterpiece, *The Brothers Karamazov* (1879–80), around the most terrible split of all in human affairs: that which leads sons to kill their father.

Dostoevsky repeatedly brings messengers for Christian redemption into the clash of ideas among and within his characters, but the Christ-like hero of *The Idiot* (1868–69) cannot connect with the existing world and ultimately becomes insane (a common fate of artists in this age). Faith is kept alive by the monastic elder Father Zosima, and tenuously transmitted through his spiritual apprentice Alyosha Karamazov to a group of young boys at the end of *The Brothers Karamazov*. We are given some sense of the redemption that he would probably have provided had he been able to complete his *Life of a Great Sinner*, a vast project that he sometimes suggested should have not three, but five parts.

The socialist dream of a secular utopia was for Dostoevsky the very opposite of his Christian ideal. He attacks in *The Possessed* the "Geneva idea" (that there has been or will be a "golden age" of perfection on earth) as the very opposite of the "Russian idea" of faith in Christ and acceptance of suffering. But in *A Raw Youth* (1875), Dostoevsky recognizes its inherent appeal:

> Marvelous dream, lofty error of mankind. The golden age is the most implausible of all the dreams that ever have been, but for it men have given up their life and all their strength, for the sake of it prophets have died and been slain, without it the people will not live and cannot die....

In drawing from the work that Dostoevsky wrote when he was first emerging from his early infatuation with romantic socialism, Janacek left behind an eerie anticipation of the direction that socialism was to take in Russia after he died in 1928. In musically re-creating Dostoevsky's memoir of his Siberian imprisonment, *Notes from the House of the Dead*, Janacek looks ahead to the Gulag Archipelago, which was then only in its early stage of development. The score provides orchestral suggestions of physical beating and clanking chains, and the prisoners ironically lament that here, indeed, everyone is equal.

The last act takes place in the prison hospital, the place of transition from a living death to death itself. But in the epilogue, although the prisoners end up returning to their cells, there is a brief lyrical tribute to freedom: "golden freedom, sweet little freedom"—one prisoner is freed, and a wounded eagle is released to the open sky. Once again, perhaps, Slavic opera was verging on prophecy. A Czech seemed to be suggesting that beyond the horrors described by Kafka lay the hopes embodied in Havel—that there would one day be light at the end of the totalitarian tunnel.

Yet, as the title of one recent Russian book has suggested, there may still be *Dark at the End of the Tunnel*. Certainly that is the message Musorgsky left behind in the lament of the holy fool at the end of *Boris*:

> Soon the enemy will come
> And darkness will fall
> Dark darkness, impenetrable...
> Grief, grief for Rus
> Weep, weep, Russian people
> Hungry people.

The good people of old Russia mount a funeral pyre at the end of *Khovanshchina*. They sink into a lake at the end of Rimsky's penultimate opera *The Tale of the Invisible City of Kitezh and the Maiden Fevronia* (1907), written in the gloomy aftermath of Russia's defeat in the Russo-Japanese War of 1904–05. And all of Russia was plunged into a "Time of Troubles" worse than any since the 17th century during the revolutionary decade between the outbreak of World War I in 1914 and the formal establishment of a new Union of Soviet Socialist Republics in 1924.

Russian music lived on, however precariously, in the Soviet era. Dmitry Shostakovich always composed with Repin's famous picture of Musorgsky before him at his writing desk. But he was subjected to repeated political pressure, and succeeded in writing only two operas—both of which were severely criticized after their first performances and not performed again for decades. *The Nose* (1930), based on Gogol's most surrealistic story, begins with a sneeze and proceeds to satirize not merely bureaucratic officialdom, but the traditional sounds and conventions of an orchestra itself. *Lady Macbeth of the Mtsensk District* (1934) is one of the great operas of the 20th century. It uses dissonance to retell with great psychological power the dark side of Russian provincial life as depicted in the powerful 19th-century novel of Nicholas Leskov.

Shostakovich survived Stalinist repression in part because he wrote mainly orchestral music. He was Russia's most prolific composer of symphonies and string quartets, writing 15 of each, and it was not always easy for even zealous censors to find an ideological message. In part, also, the texture of his symphonies was so monumental and so full of both energy and elegy that it had an irresistible appeal for Russians. But he returned towards the end of his life to link his music with texts displeasing to Soviet authorities in his 13th symphony (1962) based on Evgeny Evtushenko's poem, *Babi Yar*, denouncing Soviet anti-Semitism, and in his 14th (1969): a cycle of 11 songs dealing—as had Musorgsky in his last songs—with death.

The other great composer of the Soviet era, Sergei Prokofiev, was drawn more than Shostakovich to musical drama—and, as a result, more deeply into the web of Stalinist propaganda. He returned to Russia in 1933 after 15 years of residence abroad and spent his last 20 years in the Soviet Union. These were precisely the years of Stalin's total ascendency and greatest repression, and Prokofiev was not above composing musical pieces for special Communist festivals (cantatas for both the 20th and the 30th anniversaries of the Bolshevik Revolution in 1937 and 1947, and for Stalin's 60th birthday in 1939) and for priority propaganda campaigns. (His oratorio of 1950, *On Guard for Peace*, supported the "peace offensive" that Stalin launched as he was starting the war in Korea.)

Prokofiev wrote almost every major type of musical composition, but began, like Stravinsky, where the "mighty heap" had left off, with compositions based on pre-Christian Slavic folklore (his ballet of 1914 reworked into an orchestral *Scythian Suite* of 1916). During his long residence abroad that began in 1918, Prokofiev collaborated on productions with the two greatest Russian theatrical impresarios of the 20th century: the émigré organizer of the Ballets Russes, Sergei Diaghilev, and the pioneer of theatrical modernism in the Soviet Union, Vsevolod Meyerhold. The latter brilliantly restaged Prokofiev's first opera, *The Gambler*, in Brussels in 1929, but most of his music for the stage after returning to Russia four years later was in the politically less dangerous field of ballet.

Just as Tchaikovsky's ballets had provided a kind of fairy-tale compensation for the grimness of Alexander III's time, so did Prokofiev's brilliant ballets, *Romeo and Juliet* (1935–36) and *Cinderella* (1940–44) for the far more brutalized condition of life under Stalin. Like many of the most gifted artists of his day, he found relative creative freedom in working with children's stories (as in his "symphonic tale" of 1936, *Peter and the Wolf*).

To make his hitherto often satirical and modernist style more acceptable to a mass audience in Soviet Russia, he introduced more lyricism into his later compositions, but there was almost always an underlying strain of Musorgsky's roughness and grotesque contrasts in his compositions. Perhaps his greatest works were the series of idiosyncratic operas that he continued to work on all his life. Some of the best were never performed in his lifetime (*The Flaming Angel*, written 1917–27) or have rarely ever been seen (*Betrothal in a Monastery*, written in 1940).

Like most other Russian composers, he admired Musorgsky and sought to set Russian literary texts to music. His first opera was based on Dostoevsky's *Gambler* (first version in 1915–16, second in 1927). His last and never-completed opera was the most ambitious production ever designed for the Russian musical stage: a sprawling mega-opera *War and Peace*, based on Tolstoy's equally voluminous work.

Prokofiev began work on this project in 1941, struck by the parallels between Napoleon's invasion of Russia, the all-consuming event of Tolstoy's work, and the invasion that Hitler had launched. He wrote 13 separate scenes and introduced 60 characters, but the work had still not been completed or even trimmed down for staging at the time of his death. Through one of those strange coincidences in which Russian history abounds, Prokofiev died on the same day as Stalin—March 5, 1953.

Shostakovich and Prokofiev were both subjected to particularly vituperative criticism in Stalin's last years, but they both developed a special relationship during that period with a young cello virtuoso, Mstislav Rostropovich, who lived to play a role in the eventual downfall of the entire Soviet system. Rostropovich so dazzled Prokofiev with his playing of his long forgotten First Cello Concerto in 1947 that Prokofiev rewrote the piece for him and invited him out to live and work with him for several summers. Shostakovich wrote his only two cello concertos for Rostropovich (1959, 1966), who was in Boston recording the Second Concerto at the time of Shostakovich's death in 1975.

Rostropovich and his wife, the famed soprano Galina Vishnevskaya, had given shelter in Russia to the great writer, Alexander Solzhenitsyn, who had outraged the Communist leaders with his epic study of the Soviet concentration camp empire, *The Gulag Archipelago*. Both Solzhenitsyn and the Rostropoviches were forced out of the country and lived for many years in America—as had Prokofiev, Stravinsky, Rachmaninoff, and many others.

In August 1991, when the outcome hung in the balance during the final armed face-off between Communism and democracy, Rostropovich rushed back to stand with the forces of freedom. I was there at the time and will never forget the electric impact of his arrival on those gathered around the Russian White House who were expecting a Communist attack. It was not only the greatest performance of a great performer, but a posthumous vindication of the original assumption of the "mighty heap" that music should both come from and serve the Russian people.

The rise and fall of the Soviet Union is best reflected in a new and different art form—the cinema—which in the Communist era replaced the musical stage as the medium of the masses and the most dynamic of the arts. The master of this medium was Sergei Eisenstein, who in his last three films established with Prokofiev one of the greatest blendings of sights and sounds ever achieved in motion pictures. The ambiguous role of great art in a totalitarian state can be seen from the fact that the first of their collaborative films, *Alexander Nevsky*, strengthened allegiance to the Stalinist state, whereas the last of these films, Part II of *Ivan the Terrible*, tended to call into question that allegiance.

Eisenstein largely created the myths that legitimized Communist power. But so powerful was the new medium and so great was his artistry that his creative legacy also influenced many of those who helped undermine Communism and give Russia a new birth of freedom at the end of the 20th century.

Chapter 5

The Face of the Future: The Films of Eisenstein

Sergei Eisenstein was a protean but paradoxical genius. On the one hand, he was a brilliantly inventive director who conducted one of the most sustained and wide-ranging philosophical discussions in history about a new form of art that he himself was helping to create. He was deeply versed in a bewildering variety of both European literatures and non-European audio-visual art forms. He not only made great films often under difficult circumstances, he also sketched and wrote and taught brilliantly at the same time. He was not just being vain in describing himself as a modern Leonardo da Vinci.

On the other hand, however, Eisenstein was a lifelong adherent to the ever-changing Communist party line. His behavior towards Stalin was frequently sycophantic—his very brilliance helped mask totalitarian tyranny, and he rarely used his generally privileged position to defend or protect its victims.

Moving pictures had already become the most popular form of entertainment in Russian cities by 1917. But almost the entire native film industry fled abroad after the Revolution; and the Communists had a clear opportunity to start all over again with movies that would carry their message. From the first indoctrination films produced for the colorfully decorated *agitki* or "agitational trains" that went out into the country during the Civil War of 1918–20, movies were seen as the central art form of the Soviet era. Film was hailed as "the only book that even the illiterate can read," the bearer of "a new outlook on life...the triumph of the machine, electricity and industry." Here, moreover, was an art form that could be centrally controlled and selectively distributed.

There was little question about what the message should be for the new medium under the new conditions of Communist rule. It seemed to be a simple case of promoting the Revolution and denigrating the old order. During the protracted Civil War that followed the Communist coup in St. Petersburg in November 1917, the cerebral message of Marx gained visceral appeal for the masses through a series of outdoor demonstrations and festivals. Old monuments were draped with new symbols and slogans for the proletariat and festooned with avant-garde decor from the intelligentsia.

A great historian once suggested that the real transforming event of the French Revolution was not the widely-celebrated seizure of the Bastille on July 14, 1789, but its theatrical reenactment exactly one year later as a "Feast of Federation" on the Field of Mars in Paris. The original event had been undramatic, since the Bastille was largely deserted, and had not involved all that many people. But the reenactment was carefully staged for a far larger number of participants, who thereafter tended to remember the feast as the fact.

Something similar happened in November, 1920, on the Palace Square in Petersburg, when a great pageant,

"The Storming of the Winter Palace," was acted out on the third anniversary of the Communist seizure of power. A theatrical reenactment of the assault gave many people the idea that what had been a generally uncontested takeover late at night of a largely deserted building was in fact a carnivalesque turning-point for the human race. A Communist coup d'état came to be envisaged as a spontaneous celebratory act by the joyful masses.

Eisenstein codified this mythic image through the universally accessible medium of film. He used it to caricature the proto-democratic Provisional Government created by the previous revolution in February 1917. And he used the magic of the movies to create the implausible illusion that Marx's "alienated proletariat" had finally found a home and a new locus of legitimacy in Rastrelli's imperial Winter Palace.

Eisenstein lent a certain baroque grandeur to the Revolution by falsely representing the revolutionaries as surging to power through the long arcade and up Rastrelli's gilded Jordan staircase. He was building on the breathless account, *Ten Days That Shook the World*, by the radical American journalist John Reed. It was published in 1919 and was (in some cases still is) widely regarded as a documentary record of what actually happened.

Reed was a former Harvard cheerleader who had become an enthusiastic journalistic troubadour of strikers in Paterson, New Jersey, and of revolutionaries in Mexico. He was in Petersburg at the time, but did not actually witness most of the key events. We now know that, while writing the book, he received an enormous amount of money from the Communist International to transmit to American Communists. It was on the basis of Reed's al-

ready hyperbolic account that Eisenstein eventually codified this myth in the unforgettable visual images of his
film *October*, produced on the tenth anniversary of the
"storming of the Winter Palace."

The mythologizing of the Revolution began in
November, 1918, with an extraordinary three-day outdoor celebration on the first anniversary of what the
President of the Organizing Committee of the Petersburg Soviet had proclaimed on September 24 to be quite
simply "the greatest event in the world." All of Petersburg was redecorated as never before under the supervi-
sion of 117 artists; free food and concerts and fireworks
were provided for spectacular, open-air events centered
on the Neva River; and bridges were decorated with images of Noah's ark painted red. Many of the ceremonies
occurred on the steps of the former Stockmarket Building that jutted proudly forth into the fork of the Neva.
Both the religion and the capitalism of the old world
were being symbolically washed away by the rising tide
of Revolution.

Eisenstein was still away at the front serving with the
Red Army when all this was going on. The way that his
movies were soon to serve the new regime was foreshad-
owed on that first anniversary by the enactment on all
three days of a giant pageant called *Mystery-Bouffe* with a
cast of 100 and sets by the great "suprematist" painter of
simple geometric forms, Kazimir Malevich.

The author of this poetic pageant was the flamboyant
and irreverent Vladimir Mayakovsky. In his short life of 36
years he went through the familiar cycle of borrow-
innovate-destroy. He was a committed revolutionary from
the time of his boyhood in Georgia and a convert to "fu-

turistic" art, which rejected all previous tradition and glo-
rified industrial technology. But he invented a wildly new
kind of public persona for poets built around histrionic
public readings of staccato verse in street language that
truly did constitute (in the title of one of his works) "a slap
in the face of public taste." Disillusioned with the philis-
tinism that returned after the end of the Civil War and
disappointed in love during his subsequent wanderings
abroad, he returned to Moscow in 1928 and bitterly sati-
rized the new Soviet state in two plays, *The Bedbug* (1929)
and *The Bathhouse* (1930), before committing suicide.

But in 1918 Mayakovsky was still afire with his belief
that the Revolution would transform the entire human
condition. His poetic drama turned the biblical story of
Noah's flood into a cosmic satire suggesting that the Revolution was sweeping away all the accumulated evil of
history.

The "clean forces" of the bourgeoisie (the Pope, a German general, an American capitalist, and the political
leaders of Great Britain and France) are overthrown by
the "unclean forces" of archetypal proletarian heroes.
When the latter first appear, they are asked what nation
they represent, and they reply: "We have no nation. Our
work is our motherland."

Even more caricatured than the "clean forces" of reac-
tion is the buffoon figure in the middle, the "Menshevik-
Opportunist." He is forever brandishing an umbrella and
telling the fighting parties that there really is no cause
for conflict if they will only get together and talk things
out. Mayakovsky gives this clown-like figure the name
Soglashatel—turning the hitherto generally complimen-
tary word for "conciliator" into the kind of scornful term

of denunciation for moderates that became ritualized in later Soviet discourse.

The clean and unclean both board the ark, and the clean bring in an Abyssinian Tsar Nebus (a parody with racist overtones of the Russian word for heaven, *Nebo*) to keep the unclean in tow. But the Abyssinian eats up all the food, and the "unclean" rise up and throw him overboard singing the *Marseillaise*. They then pitch his "clean" masters into the flood, this time singing the *Internationale*.

As the flood consumes the old order, a seamstress sees a figure in the distance who she thinks is Christ. However, he proves to be simply a robust, revolutionary "man of the future." He tells them that there is no God and that they must fight to attain happiness through their own efforts. A blacksmith responds ecstatically that "There is only one way...through the clouds, through heaven [*nebo* meaning both sky and heaven] forward!"

They leave the ark and go first to Hell, which proves to be a kind of festive circus carnival of clowns and acrobats—echoing the tradition of the puppet theatre in which evil spirits are not so much satanic as comic and life-affirming. Returning at the end to a world now cleansed by the revolutionary flood, the "unclean" sing a hymn of praise—and the audience itself presumably goes forth to build the new classless society.

It is hard to appreciate today how seriously people took all this. But it had great impact both as the first political play in praise of the Communist Revolution and as an artistic tour de force. It made a deep impression on the young Eisenstein when it was revived in 1921 at the end of the Civil War to celebrate the new revolutionary feast of May Day. Eisenstein had been demobilized late in 1920 and was immersed in the radical effort to construct a new proletarian theatre. He had studied engineering and embraced Communism, but he suddenly found the role model he had never had in his dysfunctional family and unhappy youth. He went to work in 1922 for the man who had staged and directed the revival of *Mystery-Bouffe*: Vsevolod Meyerhold.

Meyerhold was quite simply the greatest theatrical innovator of the Russian 20th century. Like Mayakovsky and Eisenstein, he believed that art should be revolutionary in form as well as content. Meyerhold had acted in Chekhov plays at the Moscow Art Theatre, which had institutionalized rich naturalistic settings and emotional interpretations based on the actor's personal identification with the part being played.

Meyerhold broke with all that at the turn of the century and began doing just the opposite. He eliminated the curtain, stripped his stage, ruled out spontaneous inner emotions in favor of disciplined external motions, broke down the framed stage by thrusting the action out into the audience, and shattered traditional sensibilities by introducing into his theatre live boxing matches, machine guns, motorcycles, and flashing unfiltered lighting. He invented the so-called "wagon stage" whereby scenes were wheeled back and forth like fade-ins and fade-outs. His productions were totally controlled by a director, who arranged every element in accordance with an allegedly scientific method (his so-called "biomechanics") in which actors exemplify the basic disciplines that industrial workers would have to exercise for the building of socialism: control of movement and generation of energy.

The production of a biomechanical play was in embryo, if not in intention, a totalitarian enterprise requiring total subordination of everyone involved to the iron discipline of the director-producer.

Because Meyerhold was later denounced and executed early in 1940 after seven months of interrogation and torture, very little is left of his legacy, and almost no moving pictures exist to give us some idea of his intensely dynamic productions. Eisenstein worked closely under Meyerhold in 1922–23, which was a traumatic time both personally and professionally. He was infatuated with Meyerhold's daughter, but seems to have transferred some of his affection to the man who married her, the handsome actor Gregory Alexandrov, who, at the same time, became Eisenstein's closest lifelong friend. Eisenstein paid relatively little tribute to Meyerhold, but he did take over Meyerhold's personal archive after he was killed. Eisenstein seems to have derived from his brief but intensive tutelage under Meyerhold his belief both that the director must be in absolute control of any production and that he can use the new weapon of montage to control his audience.

Eisenstein was fascinated with the way in which Meyerhold had taken disparate elements and rearranged them so as to lead the spectator "into a desired direction (or desired mood)." The point, he wrote early in 1923, is to use "every element that can be verified and mathematically calculated to produce certain emotional shocks in the proper order within the totality."

This was the essence of montage: reassembling elements and images from the natural world into an artificial sequence that will engage the emotions and direct them towards a predetermined end. And as he moved out from Meyerhold to direct his own theatrical productions, Eisenstein tried to enliven his montage with ever more rapid changes, circus acrobatics such as tightrope walking, and the use of exaggerated on-stage horrors derived from the French tradition of *grand guignol*.

But Eisenstein was not attracting much of an audience with his "montage of attractions." He decided to break down totally the barrier between spectacle and spectator by taking a play directly into a factory and crafting it there with the aid of the real-life proletariat. Unfortunately the play *Gas Masks* was particularly bad; the setting in a foul-smelling, poorly-lit gas mask factory was even worse; and the attempt of actors to convey a message while climbing over turbines and running along catwalks was worst of all.

In wandering around the factory and wondering why this experiment had been such a failure, Eisenstein discovered the faces that lay behind the gas masks and beyond Meyerhold's "theatre of masks." He became fascinated with faces he had never seen close up before: the natural faces of real workers doing real work. He noticed—and loved—their individuality. They were no longer just an abstract "proletariat" or an undifferentiated mass of "caviar." They were the faces of the new Russia. Eisenstein instinctively felt that their various expressions could make his "sequence of attractions" genuinely attractive. But an altogether new medium of expression was needed—not an old one inserted into the new world of machines, electricity and perpetual motion of the factory. The new art form was now rising out of those very elements: the moving picture.

"An explosion occurred within Eisenstein," his friend Marie Seton wrote of this moment. Eisenstein himself noted that, having taken his cart full of attractions to the workers, "the cart fell to pieces and the driver dropped into the cinema." He immediately plunged into a fever of innovative composition with almost no sleep—rather like that which Musorgsky had experienced in writing the *Night on Bald Mountain* and the Kromy Forest scene of *Boris*. Out of this white-hot burst of creativity came the outline for his first movie, *Strike*, and the grandiose vision of undertaking a seven-part film epic to be called *Toward Dictatorship*. It was to trace the Russian revolutionary tradition up to the Communist victory of 1917 and the establishment of what Marx and Lenin had called the "dictatorship of the proletariat." *Strike* was originally conceived as the fifth episode in this cycle.

This vision of a great revolutionary epic basically defined the entire first half of Eisenstein's meteoric career as a filmmaker. He produced in rapid succession a series of silent films that depict key stages in the rise of Russia's deified Revolution. *Strike* (1924) tells the story of a generic industrial strike and its brutal repression in Tsarist times; *The Battleship Potemkin* (1925) describes a heroic mutiny during Russia's first revolution in 1905; *October* describes the Communist coup in Petersburg in 1917; and *The Old and The New* (originally entitled *The General Line*, 1929) attempted to translate into the language of cinema the command to collectivize agriculture issued at the 14th Communist Party Congress. This, his last silent movie, tells the story of how a peasant woman brings people into an agricultural cooperative and forges a link with an urban tractor driver. Illustrations of urban and rural productivity are intercut, and the arrival of a cream separator is transformed into a scene of erotic ecstacy. Neither that picture nor the frequent humor in the film bore, of course, any relation to the grim reality of forced collectivization that was already in evidence by the time of the film's delayed release.

Eisenstein had brought into being in the space of five short years a new medium, a new method and a new mythology. Russia was once again experiencing a "culture of explosion"—and of metaphysical overload—as it entered into the familiar cycle of massive borrowing and stunning innovation followed by breakdown in yet another new form of art.

Eisenstein borrowed mainly from Hollywood, to which he came in 1930, when the advent of Stalinist repression and of sound film caused him to rethink his artistry and to prepare for the very different films he was to produce in the late 1930s and 1940s.

The pre-revolutionary and early post-revolutionary Russian cinema had been under predominantly European influence, the French firm of Pathé having been the original investor in the Russian industry. But Eisenstein had long been fascinated by Charlie Chaplin and the slapstick vitality of American silent films; and, at the crucial point of Eisenstein's transition from plays to films, he had discovered the basic model for his own epic work in D. W. Griffith's *Intolerance*.

Griffith had developed his own brilliant montage of contrasting images in his famed epic of the Civil War, *Birth of a Nation*, but its racism subjected his dramatic narrative to sharp criticism and, in some places, to censorship. Outraged by this perceived attack on his creative freedom and also by the bloodshed of World War I, Griffith produced his even more spectacular and ambitious *Intolerance*. Meyerhold had implanted in Eisenstein the idea that a succession of images should be "musical rather than realistic." Griffith now presented him with living proof that the music could be majestically polyphonic.

Griffith's film was constructed like a fugue, intercutting episodes from ancient Babylon, Christ's crucifixion, France during the religious wars, and a contemporary story. The whole was linked together by the recurrent image of the beautiful Lillian Gish rocking a cradle, illustrating Walt Whitman's lines "out of the cradle, endlessly rocking, Uniter of Here and Hereafter." Filmed in part from balloons and on a set that spread over more than 250 acres in Hollywood, Griffith's film brought all four elements and his cast of thousands together in a spectacular finale that was in many ways the mother of all movie melodramas.

If Griffith provided the technical model for a heroic epic in the new medium, the Communist Revolution provided for Eisenstein the positive message that was thought to be missing from Griffith's two pathbreaking but ultimately "bourgeois" films. Eisenstein's *Strike* develops simple geometric patterns and Daumier-like caricatures to make more visually compelling the simple contrast in *Mystery-Bouffe* between good and evil. Figuratively as well as literally, Eisenstein's revolutionary epics were entirely black and white.

The powerful final scene of *Strike* superimposes the image of a steer bleeding to death over a moving mass of suffering strikers. The most famous of all his scenes is that in *Potemkin* which shows Cossack troops slaughtering peaceful people on the steps of Odessa during the Revolution of 1905. Both the glory of a parade and the humanity of the Tsarist army are stripped away as an old woman is stepped on by jackboots and a baby carriage is detached from a mother to hurtle down the stairway of death. *October* depicts the final triumph of the revolution, as idealized revolutionaries dethrone the Provisional Government and shatter all the bottles in the wine cellar of the decadent old order. They then celebrate with an uncharacteristically alcohol-free carnival of their own—as if in response to the poet Alexander Blok's rewriting of a line from a revolutionary song: "Go lads—no need of wine."

Revolutionaries never show cowardice or vacillation, and counter-revolutionaries never endure suffering or show magnanimity in Eisenstein's mythological movies. But Eisenstein began to have difficulty in serving simply as a straightforward cheerleader when revolutionaries in power began massive programs of social coercion. Eisenstein's attempt to support collectivization of the peasantry in *The Old and the New* was less crudely didactic than his preceding sagas, and accordingly subjected to far more criticism. Eisenstein's last effort to create a film in support of collectivization, *Bezhin Meadow* of 1935–37, was confiscated and destroyed before it was ever released for public viewing. Eisenstein had taken the title from Turgenev but his subject matter from the story of the young Communist activist Pavlik Morozov who was killed after informing on his father and became a hero-martyr of Stalinist propaganda during the brutal years of forced collectivization. Eisenstein produced a somewhat idealized version of this grisly story. The boy is defending for the state the harvest of a collective farm, against the selfish resistance of his reactionary kulak father, who ends up killing his son.

By the mid-1930s Eisenstein was largely out of work and favor in the Soviet Union. He had for some time been reaching both outside Russia for fresh artistic inspiration and inside himself for deeper self-understanding. He had added Chinese to his long interest in Japanese art and undertaken a vast Mexican filming project that was never completed. The entries in his diaries grew longer, and the volume and variety of his sketches steadily increased.

Eisenstein had been specially fascinated by Mexico and the haunting suggestion that some mysteriously wonderful pre-Columbian view of life lay hidden within the silent rural masses and behind the indecipherable Mayan pictograms.

Eisenstein's infatuation with archaic Mexico was in many ways a continuation and culmination of the secular modernist search for some source of art anterior to Christianity. Pagan subject matter had become increasingly important to Russian composers. One of the most original works of the "mighty heap" was Rimsky-Korsakov's "magical opera-ballet" *Mlada* (first performed 1892), which celebrated the ancient beliefs and rituals of the pagan Eastern Slavs. Prokofiev wrote a number of important pre-war works on pagan topics, and, of course, musical modernism was largely born in 1913 with the first performance of Stravinsky's *Rite of Spring,* which purported to re-create a pagan ritual.

Eisenstein quite properly saw himself as looking back

to the archaic past for material to sustain his faith in a utopian future. Mysticism about Mexico played for him the same role that Egyptomania played for artistic acolytes of the French Revolution. They brought obelisks into Paris as antique symbols of freedom and contended that Notre Dame Cathedral covered over a pre-existent shrine for "Notre Isis."

Eisenstein wanted to salvage the Communist view of the world from the paranoid purge atmosphere of his Communist motherland. He even played for a long time with the bizarre idea of making Karl Marx's long and turgid treatise, *Das Kapital*, into a movie.

In his brief stay in Hollywood from June through December of 1930, Eisenstein had come up with a marvellous set of ideas for films that would use all of the latest photographic and sound techniques to depict the emptiness of American capitalism: its urban life in inhuman skyscrapers (*The Glass House*), its subhuman materialism exhibited in the gold rush (*Sutter's Gold*), and its degradation of human relationships (*An American Tragedy*). None of these proposals was put into production because, as David O. Selznick dryly observed of Eisenstein's scenario for filming Theodore Dreiser's classic novel, it "cannot possibly offer anything but a most miserable two hours to millions of happy-minded young Americans."

What his stay in America offered Eisenstein, however, was a chance to explore the meaning of life rather than just go on promoting the cause of Communism. His scenario for *The Glass House* was in many ways a visualization of Eugene Zamyatin's novel of 1924, *We*, the first great anti-utopian novel and the progenitor of *Brave New*

World and *Animal Farm*. It would have been unthinkable in the USSR to make a film out of a satirical work that had been directed at—and immediately denounced by— the Soviet Communist establishment.

Fascinated by the new expressive possibilities of the sound film, Eisenstein developed a new theory of "vertical montage," and illustrated it by drawing up in his notebooks in the winter of 1934–35 an elaborate scenario of how he would handle the final death scene of the revolutionary hero in André Malraux's novel, *Man's Fate*. Ernest Hemingway had called this scene (in which the hero gives two of his comrades his supply of poison in case they cannot endure the torture that they will have to undergo after his death) one of the greatest moments in 20th century literature. The execution is announced not visually but with a train whistle, each member of the group was to be given "its own musical line," and the lines and pictures would all come together at the end to create "the greatest fugue ever made." Eisenstein was adding American hyperbole to Russian megalomania—accepting Hemingway's judgment as oracular and the fugal structure of Griffith's *Intolerance* as an ideal archetype.

His scenario for *An American Tragedy* proposed using the new polyphonic relationship between sound and picture not to drive home the ideological point that the conditions of capitalism produced the tragic ending, but rather to provide the "psychic drumming" of an inexorably advancing tragedy. The loutish social climber who first impregnated and then drowned the poor working girl was to be speeded on his way to their final, fatal meeting by "concrete music" more than by pictures. The clicking of train wheels would suggest the rhythmic repetition of the Russian words for "Kill! Kill!" (*ubei! ubei!*). The polyphony was to be resolved by a lengthy train whistle, after which the prospective murderer descends from the train, and the fateful ending unfolds.

The prolonged whistle of a moving machine had become, for the anti-clerical Eisenstein, the modern, secular surrogate for a bell ringing in a stationary church. It summons everyone to leave behind the clashing tensions of ordinary life and enter into a redemptive ritual about to begin. This was expressed by the sustained image of a boat whistle blowing steam in *Potemkin* even before there was a soundtrack, and such sounds were to have figured prominently in *Bezhin Meadow*.

Unable to produce a film in Hollywood and under suspicion of being a Communist agent, Eisenstein left the United States for Mexico in December, 1930, to embark on a vast filming project that, in effect, engaged his energies on three different levels.

At the first and most superficial level, Eisenstein was continuing to propagate the progressive, revolutionary cause. Even before Russia, Mexico had produced a socialist revolution in 1910 which had led to the adoption of a radical constitution in January, 1917. Eisenstein was fascinated by the leftist artists in Mexico who were painting refreshingly simple, yet truly monumental murals. He began thinking of his own films as "moving frescoes (for we also work on walls!)." He travelled and worked with these politically active Mexican artists, and appears to have believed that his own dualistic revolutionary view of the world could be reinforced by juxtaposing the primitive popular art of Mexico to the repressive Catholicism that had been superimposed over it.

At the deeper, creative level, Eisenstein was working with the model of a great cinematic fugue that Griffith had provided in *Intolerance*. The mega-film that he saw himself producing was to interweave narrative segments from a variety of different regions of Mexico and periods of its history. Each part was to be dedicated to a Mexican artist. The project was woefully underfunded and never completed, but it produced a magnificent body of raw footage that revealed—for the first time clearly in his public work—that there was yet another, more personal level to Eisenstein's creative life.

This third level involved sex and religion: two of the subjects that were most anathema to the atheistic and puritanical culture that Stalin was imposing on Russia in the 1930s. Eisenstein had been reading Freud for many years, had undergone psychoanalysis in California, and had concluded that his own repressed and lonely personal life was the result of hatred for both his biological father (an assimilated Jew who had left Russia after fighting with the Whites in the Civil War) and his artistic father, Meyerhold (an assimilated Prussian who had changed his name from Karl-Theodor Kasimir to Vsevolod only when he formally took Russian citizenship). Eisenstein compared Meyerhold to Freud as a brilliant innovator who, however, never fully revealed his secrets to his protégés, just as his own father had never told him anything about sex.

"God willed that in questions of 'secrecy' my spiritual papa should be just like my biological one," he lamented. The phrase "How can I tell that to a child?" appears four times—always in German—in his memoirs. He seemed to have burst forth into a delayed and libidinous adulthood in Mexico. His voluminous Mexican drawings were often too erotic to be permitted back by mail into the United States, and he seems to have enriched his imaginative if not his physical existence with a newfound sexual expressiveness that was at times polymorphous or bisexual, but basically homoerotic.

Eisenstein appears also to have had something of an Oedipus complex towards his possessive mother whom he basically disliked but with whom he lived at several points even in his adult life. Vasily Rozanov, the great writer of the late Imperial period who more than anyone else introduced eros into Russian literature, had imagined himself literally returning to his fetal state and asking not to be born "because it is warm enough in here." Eisenstein avidly read Otto Rank's then famous book, *The Trauma of Birth*, which took to absurd extremes the idea that people were forever seeking to return to their mothers' wombs. He saw the same essential idea reflected in the biblical tale of Jonah, in the myth of the Minotaur in the labyrinth, and in modern detective stories. All of these were "focused on the primal quest to find the supreme truth within some secret and inaccessible space, the archetype of which was the maternal womb."

In his own introspective search for "supreme truth," he began to dwell as never before on the basic mystery of life and death and on the burgeoning new anthropological literature on religion. He was an atheist and had always depicted Orthodox Christianity in the most hostile way despite (or perhaps because of) his family's long record of patronizing the Alexander Nevsky Monastery in St. Petersburg. But he became intrigued—morbidly, perhaps even masochistically—with what he saw as the

brutality of Catholicism in Mexico even as he was falling in love with Mexico's mysterious Indian religions. He seems to have been seduced by everything in this strange archaic world where religious, narcotic, and sexual ecstasy all could be experienced. He spoke of his never finished film project there as a "poem of love, death and immortality."

When he moved back to Russia in 1932, his land was in the throes of convulsive change. He seemed to look even beyond the womb in search of "the primal unity of everything"—something that could somehow reunite the old and the new, male and female, the divinity with the animality of mankind. But he was not able to film any of his efforts to interweave—and thus help unify—old and new Russia: neither his satire bringing medieval boyars into the modern Soviet Union (MMM), nor his epic of the building of a Stalinist project in the Central Asian desert (*The Great Ferghana Canal*), nor a projected documentary on the 800-year history of Moscow. Meanwhile, his friends began to disappear into the gulags, and he himself was forced into humiliating self-criticism of his *Bezhin Meadow*.

The filmmaker who had put a human face on the revolutionary cause and urged his countrymen to believe in a Communist future had become a frightened supplicant for survival. He asked to be allowed to do a film on either the Spanish Civil War or the original formation of the Red Army in 1917. After a long period of unresponsive silence from Soviet officials, they assigned him a topic, most of a cast, and a political watchdog to guard against unauthorized changes in the script.

In this unpromising and unfamiliar situation, Eisenstein began working in the fall of 1937 on what was to become one of the greatest movies of all time: *Alexander Nevsky*. Gone was all the introspection and irony of his recent wander-years. Gone, too, was all effort to depict current Russian reality or transmit Marxist ideas. This was a purely romantic, historical epic about a great 13th-century warrior-saint who rallied a divided Russia to repulse invasion by the Teutonic knights—unifying and rescuing the Russian people in their darkest hour.

With Soviet leaders worried about the rise of Nazi Germany and the masses increasingly bombarded with nationalistic symbols and exhortations, Russia was ripe for a roiling patriotic drama. Eisenstein originally planned to call it *Rus*. He used his proven skills at legitimizing the good guys with earthy humanity and attributing caricatured inhumanity to the bad guys. But it was now a case of foreigners vs. Russians rather than workers vs. capitalists. Eisenstein derived images of grandeur for his great battle scenes from a reading of Milton's *Paradise Lost*. And the spectacular musical score by Prokofiev gave the film an almost operatic quality.

The conflict is represented visually as between bearded recognizably human faces of Russians and metallically masked German knights whose faces are rarely seen, and musically between the rhythmic, often melodic folk music of the defenders and the dissonant clanging of the invaders' swords and armor. The great charge of the knights begins in Prokofiev's score before it is recognizable on Eisenstein's screen. The charge ends with the knights' sinking into a Russian lake as their excessive armor breaks through the ice.

This famous scene brilliantly plays to the unstated but

instinctive Russian belief that nature is ultimately on their side against the unnatural advantages of invaders. And, of course, it seemed to anticipate the later Russian experience in World War II when the metallic might of German tanks was ultimately defeated by a combination of grass-roots heroism, punishing winters, and the exhausting expanse of the Russian land.

No sooner had Eisenstein finished the film and received acclaim within and beyond the Soviet Union, than Stalin signed the Nazi-Soviet pact in August, 1939, and took *Nevsky* out of circulation. The ever-compliant Eisenstein turned back to the theatre and created lavish sets for a new production of Wagner's *Die Walküre* in the Bolshoi Theatre in Moscow in 1940.

When Hitler invaded Russia in June, 1941, *Nevsky* was circulated anew and Eisenstein was assigned to produce a patriotic encore. This time he was given the unprecedented privilege of writing his own script and drawing on a very generous budget. When the German tanks advanced close to Moscow late in 1941, he and his entire production were moved to distant Alma Ata in Kazakhstan, and they were permitted—and at times urgently enjoined—to continue their work all during the war.

This was to be Eisenstein's last film—and a Herculean attempt to produce yet another great Russian trilogy in yet another medium. In terms of the creative cycle that we have found to recur with each cultural explosion in Russian history, Eisenstein had borrowed from foreign models and then proceeded to do something wildly original with the newly adopted art form. He was now moving into the megalomanic phase of attempting to produce a redemptive project for Russia. It would ultimately prove to be unrealizable and would unintentionally begin the process of fragmentation and decline for the new medium.

The assigned subject was Ivan the Terrible. The task was to create an inspirational patriotic film for the war effort. The problem—and the opportunity—was that Stalin had increasingly identified himself with the figure of Ivan.

Stalin had placed pictures of Ivan the Terrible and Peter the Great on the walls of his Kremlin office along with those of Marx and Lenin in the course of the 1930s. Peter had been lionized in a two-part film series in 1937 and 1939 in a swaggering, straightforward manner that pleased Stalin and became the model for historical films. But the epic on Peter was based on an historical novel that had already won a Stalin prize, and it had depicted the relatively simple story of a ruthless but effective modernizer. No comparably acceptable literary interpretation of Ivan the Terrible had appeared in the Soviet era, and no consensus existed in the earlier historical literature about what, if anything, Ivan accomplished beyond the capture of Kazan. When Rimsky-Korsakov returned in 1899 to the time of Ivan in *The Tsar's Bride*, he solved the problem of how to represent Ivan by letting him appear on stage for only one brief, non-speaking moment.

Historical paintings of Ivan offered no clear guidance (as they had for the film on Peter the Great). Secular portraiture had been forbidden in Ivan's time. Subsequent pictorial representations of him ranged from the sublime (in the icon of "The Church Victorious" and the sanctuary fresco in Sviiazhsk) through the enigmatic (in Mark Antokolsky's brooding bronze statue of 1871 which the admiring Tsar Alexander II had put on view in the Hermitage) to the grotesque (in Ilya Repin's blood-red canvas of 1885 depicting a crazed Ivan cuddling the son he had just murdered) (see illustration 28). But what made any drama about Ivan the Terrible particularly terrifying at this time was that no one knew exactly what the all-powerful Stalin expected from the project.

One political imperative was, however, clear at the outset. Eisenstein's film had to present a happy ending and a heroic Ivan. Stalin had personally intervened to change the original ending of *Nevsky* so that the hero did not die. Eisenstein worked hard to get Nicholas Cherkasov for the part of Ivan. Cherkasov was a powerful figure in the Communist Party and a politically correct member of the Supreme Soviet who had already played Nevsky for Eisenstein and acted in the well-received project on Peter the Great.

Eisenstein also had to incorporate into his technique a great deal of the very acting style that he had originally rebelled against: the realistic, declamatory style of the Moscow Art Theatre. The high priest of the alternate, modernist approach, his old mentor Vsevolod Meyerhold, and his actress-wife had both been murdered at the end of Stalin's purges in 1940. Eisenstein clearly did not want to risk sharing their fate.

In the mid-1930s, Stalin had made the muddled doctrine of "socialist realism" obligatory for all the arts. This concept required an objective portrayal of reality in terms understandable to the average man and, at the same time, a plot and cast of characters that would inspire support for the "building of socialism." By the end of that blood-soaked decade this set of contradictory expectations had been further vulgarized into a theatrical, totalitarian cult of the all-wise leader. As a former seminarian, Stalin created atheistic equivalents for the two generic outdoor happenings that had traditionally taken Russian Orthodoxy out of church buildings into public places for special occasions: the pilgrimage and the procession.

Pilgrimages were conducted every day just outside the Kremlin walls. Endless lines filed by the wonder-working remains of the deified corpse of Lenin, whose authority was used to rationalize everything his successors did. Lenin's mummified body lay underground with folded hands in his Red Square mausoleum like the original Russian saints in the Kievan Monastery of the Caves.

Processions to end all processions were held on the great feast days of the world's first atheistic state (May 1 and November 7). Endless displays of metallic might streamed through Red Square along with uniformed children bearing icons of their Great Leader. They all filed reverently past the ritually ordered icon screen of Communist Party leaders atop the Lenin Mausoleum. The officials stood, as the icon screen often did, directly over the buried body of the founding holy man.

The new Stalinist disciples that emerged from all the blood-letting purges of the 1930s made their infrequent collective public appearances on such occasions—and were neurotically anxious to know whether their assigned places were getting nearer or farther away from the Leader. Exactly where they stood could be, literally, a

matter of life or death. They were all worshipfully inclined—as had been the figures on the main "prayer row"
of the classical icon screen—towards the incarnation of
God who had saved them, and now stood at the center of
the row.

Stalin, who in the 1930s conducted the greatest
pogrom of Christians in the 20th century, put himself, in
effect, in the place of Christ as the "savior of strength"
(*Spas v silakh*) and of "the penetrating eye"(*yaroe oko*) at
the center of this new outdoor icon screen.

Russian culture had moved all the way from the majestically simple Spas that Rublev had anonymously painted
for a village church to what many believed to be the en-
thronement in the Moscow Kremlin of the Antichrist.
Whereas Rublev created an authentically spiritual art out
of a life of silence, Stalin had destroyed most of that older
art and created a culture of emperor worship in which silence was not permitted. The face on the firewood had
been replaced by the face of fire itself.

We now know that Stalin had been carefully coached
in the 1930s by a leading actor from the Moscow Art
Theatre on how to intensify a sense of mysterious dread
among those who came into his presence. Long pauses
as if to suggest profound reflection were to be followed
by short, often deliberately ambiguous pronouncements.
Puffing a pipe was the stage prop for increasing suspense.
Occasional brief smiles or sudden, gratuitous favors provided fleeting moments of comic relief or illusory hope
that only heightened the subsequent feeling of fearful
uncertainty—and increased dependence on the all-
powerful Leader.

Like Lenin, Stalin attached special importance to

movies as the medium of the masses and art form of the modern age. He often personally previewed a film in the presence of everyone who had had anything to do with it. They were all left in extended uncertainty as to whether the new Nero would give the all-determining up or down signal. The stakes were enormous, and Stalin seemed to want to prove that he was the best actor of all by delaying his judgment as everyone squirmed and sweated in agonizing silence.

Eisenstein was exempted from all of this and put in a specially privileged position. He was, in effect, made part of the war effort. He was able to work in relative freedom far from Moscow with ample support. He had a dream team of collaborators led by Eduard Tisse and Sergei Prokofiev, widely believed to be, respectively, Russia's greatest living composer of photographic shots and of musical sounds. Out of all of this, Eisenstein was expected to create another masterpiece, and he initially seemed to have succeeded when Part I of *Ivan the Terrible* was released to national and international acclaim in January, 1945, just as the war was drawing to a victorious close.

He had produced a powerful drama showing how Ivan had suffered grievous personal loss and loneliness in order to defend and unify the Russian people. Eisenstein had drawn fresh artistic ideas from immersion in yet another rich array of masters from other media: the tragic grandeur of Shakespearean historical dramas, the agitated paintings of El Greco, and the labyrinth of *leit motifs* in Wagnerian opera. He had brooded long and hard over the way in which both Pushkin and Musorgsky had portrayed Tsar Boris Godunov. And he had combined the Old Russian idea of inverse perspective with Meyerhold's modernist invention of the wagon stage to thrust a play-within-a-play forward into the audience within the film and the spectators in the theatre.

The play was one of the oldest in Russia: the so-called Furnace Act which dramatized the miraculous rescue of the three Hebrew children from the fiery furnace into which the Babylonian King Nebuchadnezzar had put them as punishment for maintaining their faith. By setting the play in a dark Cathedral and pushing out into the foreground the angelic figures of the white-clad, softly singing youths, he lent a certain majesty to a ritual that had not been publicly performed for years in the Soviet Union. At the same time, he provided a first hint for the war-weary Russian people that their current ruler might be more a Babylonian tyrant imposing suffering than a Russian hero enduring it.

Eisenstein had described Prokofiev's score as "a cathedral of sound" and likened his own creation of a unitary film out of so many complex ingredients to the building of a cathedral. The difficulty was that it was dimly lit, and that the gargoyles seemed to be taking it over.

To be sure, Eisenstein identifies Ivan with the sun symbol, includes spacious battle scenes showing the conquest of Kazan, and ends his epic expansively with Ivan reaching the sea and supplicants coming to him across the snow-covered plain begging him to return to Moscow. But most of the action occurs inside dark religious buildings and depicts court intrigues against Ivan that lead to the murder of both his mother and his wife. The message was heroic, but the images often seemed grotesque.

The atmosphere of claustrophobic interiors, morose

plotting and caricatured conspirators reached near-neurotic intensity in Part II of Eisenstein's projected trilogy. Entitled "The Conspiracy of the Boyars," it showed how Ivan created his hooded private army of *Oprichniki* (the new "separate estate" that directly served the Tsar) in order to save the state and crush the conspirators.

Eisenstein revived some of the carnivalesque features of the early revolutionary theatre to give vitality to his dazzling depiction of the Oprichniki. The great scene of Ivan the Terrible's consorting with them begins with a jump cut from black-and-white into color. Like the Russian abstract expressionist painter, Vasily Kandinsky, Eisenstein attributes symbolic significance to each color: blue represents heaven; red, vengeance; black, death; and gold, debauchery. The host of symbolic objects and geometric framing patterns that are folded into Eisenstein's polyphonic interplay of words, colors, and sounds fascinate—but may in the end tend to overwhelm—the viewer.

The climax of Part II is the mock crowning of the effeminate young Vladimir, son of Efrosinia, Ivan's aunt and the leader of the conspiracy against him. In a carnival-like inversion of roles Ivan crowns the pitiful Vladimir, which leads Efrosinia's assassin mistakenly to kill Vladimir instead of Ivan. The half-crazed Efrosinia coddles her dead son in much the way Ivan does his in Repin's famed painting. She sings him an eerie folksong reminiscent of the scene at the very end of Tchaikovsky's great opera, *Mazepa*, in which the heroine loses her mind, then cradles the dying hero in a similar pietà-like position and sings him an unearthly lullaby.

All of this was too much for Stalin and his leaden cultural bureaucracy. The film was denounced at the Communist Party Congress in August, 1946, and Eisenstein was forced into another round of humiliating self-criticism. He was never able to show Part II or to film anything else. During the night of February 9–10, 1948, just a few days after his 50th birthday, he died—as he had largely lived—alone.

There has been a tendency in post-Communist Russia to describe Eisenstein as a closet dissident, and the two specific criticisms that the cultural commissars made of Eisenstein's last work were clearly not entirely unjustified. Ivan the Terrible *was* given some "Hamlet-like" moments of indecisive introspection by Eisenstein, and the Oprich-nina *was* depicted in ways that bore some resemblance to the Ku Klux Klan (particularly its positive depiction in Griffith's *Birth of a Nation*).

There is sly hidden criticism of the Soviet system in many of his works. Even in *Potemkin* the reactionary priest slips in a wink at the viewer. Eisenstein was a great and dedicated teacher throughout his life, and seems to have imparted views to his protégés that were critical of, if not contrary to, the reigning ideology. Moreover, his artistic inventiveness was so many-sided and seminal that he posthumously exercised powerful stylistic influence on young filmmakers like Tengiz Abuladze who later helped bring an end to Communism in Russia.

But the inescapable fact is that in his life as a public artist he created a largely fictitious mythology about the Russian revolutionary tradition and consistently worked within and for the ever-changing line of the ruling Com-munist Party. Though divergent ideas are embedded within his work, he never basically deviated from his servility to Soviet power.

His mentor Meyerhold had insisted that actors control their bodies in his "biomechanical" productions, so that the all-powerful director could control the audience's involvement in the flow of scenes that would assure the predetermined impact of a play. Eisenstein translated this inherently authoritarian idea to the cinema, but his aim was to help direct an entire nation towards the goals of the Soviet state. The net effect, however unintended, was to contribute to the totalitarian controls that would eventually silence him.

In his last years, when he was no longer able to make films, Eisenstein began semi-secretly to work on a study of the relationship between the two founding fathers of Russian literature, Pushkin and Gogol. He seems to have believed that Gogol's well-known veneration for Pushkin was in fact a homosexual infatuation, and that all of Gogol's writings were in some way replies to, or at least affected by, this unrequited love.

Leaving aside whether such a project tells us anything of importance about either Gogol or Eisenstein, this and the other preoccupations of Eisenstein's last years suggest that he was seeking resolution in his native Russia of some of the personal problems that he had previously explored inconclusively during his time in the United States and Mexico. His core concerns were distinctively Russian and ultimately religious.

In the fragmentary still photographs that are nearly all that have survived from the never-filmed Part III, there are elements of what would have been the climactic scene of his trilogy. Ivan is in a cathedral talking to a giant painting of Christ at the center of a fresco of the Last Judgment (see illustration 29). Ivan asks Christ if he was not justified in imposing suffering on many individuals in order to alleviate the suffering of the Russian people as a whole. Christ does not answer, and Ivan hurls his staff at him.

Eisenstein may have intended to mention the names of Stalin's rather than Ivan's victims in that scene. Had he lived on to see Stalin's final spasm of post-war repression, Eisenstein might well have been purged himself and/or have chosen finally to speak out.

In his last days, Eisenstein was still in search of some primal unity which would resolve the divisions and contradictions of life. His late-blooming interest in the deeply religious Gogol and Dostoevsky above all other Russian writers and his fascination with cathedrals seem to suggest that he was seeking at the end some way to overcome or transcend his lifelong hostility to the Russian Orthodox Church.

And yet, in the last analysis, the closest he actually came to finding inner peace and resolving his sense of loneliness and division seems to have been by dissolving himself spiritually into the very undifferentiated crowd that he had tried so hard to individualize in his early movies. Vasily Rozanov has described how he was seduced by watching a seemingly unending military parade pass through Petersburg in 1903:

> My "ego" was blown like a piece of down into the whirlwind of that enormousness and that crowd....
> All of a sudden, I started to feel that I was not only afraid of, but fascinated by them.... I did not look

at any specific face [but] to a mass ... [which] invoked in me the purely womanish sentiment of spineless obedience.

Eisenstein seems to have felt something similar after returning to Stalinist Russia from libidinous Mexico. One observer has described it as an erotic attachment to "the mob's unitary, undiscriminating, sexless and constantly regenerating body." It might also be seen as "spineless," even "womanish," obedience to anyone who was able to control and lead that mass as totally as Meyerhold had controlled the human body in his "biomechanical" theatrical performances.

Eisenstein explained with a certain gusto his growing emphasis on the grotesque and violent:

> In my films, crowds of people are mowed down, hooves trample the skulls of farm laborers buried up to their necks ... children are crushed on the Odessa staircase, thrown from rooftops, and left to die by their own parents. ... It seems not at all coincidental that for a number of years the ruler of my thoughts and my favorite hero has been Ivan the Terrible.

This identification was made stronger by Eisenstein's belief that Ivan, like himself, had suffered terrifying experiences in childhood. Eisenstein seemed to believe of both Ivan and Stalin that "adult affairs demanded brutality, and anyone who had been prepared by childhood trauma had a headstart."

Having borrowed a new medium from the West and

then produced stunning innovations of his own, Eisenstein did not live to see the breakup and breakdown of the Soviet cinema in the late Stalin years.

The most celebrated films of that era were vulgarly propagandistic. War movies emphasized Stalin's infallible leadership and/or the deceptive treachery of Russia's wartime allies.

The best Soviet war movie of the late Stalin era, *The Battle of Stalingrad*, had unprecedented credit lines listing the names of the photographers who had been killed filming the chilling documentary footage of that great military contest.

In the dramatized part of the original version, we approach the Kremlin through the clouds somewhat in the way Hitler had been shown approaching Nuremberg in Leni Riefenstahl's classic Nazi propaganda film, *The Triumph of the Will*. Nothing seems to be able to stop the German advance, and Russia's generals are quivering in fear and indecision. Stalin enters bathed in a nimbus of light. There is a long and agonizing silence and a slow tracking shot across a vast map of Russia. When the camera reaches Stalingrad, the Great Leader's fist comes crashing down with the command *Nado napadat!* (We must attack!) There is an immediate jump cut to a mass firing of rockets. The tide has turned. Victory is assured.

This magnificently mythological sequence was subsequently watered down to a simple telephone call from Stalin saying "Let's go!" Stalin's heirs awkwardly tried to shed the excesses of his "cult of personality" while holding on to the abundant fruits they had harvested from it. Nikita Khrushchev criticized some of Stalin's early crimes against Communists before a secret party gathering in

1956, but could not get Stalin's body out of the mausoleum next to Lenin until he dragged in supernatural testimony from an old Communist woman at a party gathering five years later.

> Yesterday I asked Ilich [the patronymic of Lenin] for advice, and it was as if he stood before me alive and said, "I do not like being next to Stalin, who inflicted so much harm on the Party."

The Communist Party had become the self-serving, self-perpetuating bureaucracy of a largely parasitic "new class." Russia continued to be ruled by the aging protégés and beneficiaries of the late Stalin era for a third of a century after Stalin's death. The public culture of the USSR went into steady decline. The quantity of films increased, but the quality decreased. It seemed fitting that Nicholas Virta, who wrote the script for *The Battle of Stalingrad*, later wrote a script for *The Fall of Pompeii* after Stalin died.

The ruling Communist oligarchy tried to defend their legitimacy by insisting on the purity of the original Revolution. They were posthumously aided by Eisenstein in making this case. So vivid and familiar was his idealized chronicle of the Revolution that people remembered his fiction as reality. Soviet television repeatedly broadcast excerpts from Eisenstein's films as if they were newsreel footage. The flood of idealized pictorial propaganda at the time of the 50th anniversary of the Communist Revolution (1967) and the 100th anniversary of Lenin's birth (1970) led many to assume that Lenin was better than people had been willing to believe even if Stalin may have been worse. This "balanced" view was widely accepted even in the West. Few seemed to have suspected then that hundreds of key documents revealing the darker side of Lenin had been kept out of all of the many Soviet editions of his "complete" works.

Soviet totalitarianism was a phenomenon without precedent in human affairs. So, too, has been the attempt to build a democracy following the Communist collapse. Russia has plunged into yet another "Time of Troubles"—and confronted once again the challenge to be creative in a new field with which they have had little prior experience.

Chapter 6

The Human Reality: Facing Freedom

Film once again acquired an important social role with the coming of Gorbachev, glasnost, and a new generation in the mid-1980s. The brief literary thaw under Khrushchev had provided a foretaste of what was to come with three remarkable films that put a human face on the war effort. *Ballad of a Soldier* (1957), *The Cranes are Flying* (1960), and *My Name is Ivan* (1962) all treated the war not as an epic seen from on high, but as the simple story of suffering at the human level. In all three films the camera repeatedly maps human faces rather than the contours of battlefields. A mother rushes through the wheat fields for a brief last moment with her son on a fleeting furlough; a young girl weaves her way through a fleet of departing tanks searching vainly for the fiancé she will never get to marry; a young orphaned boy stares at us from a scorched forest.

The long "time of stagnation" under Leonid Brezhnev continued during the brief reign of his aged, ailing, and short-lived successors, Yury Andropov and Konstantin Chernenko. There was ferment beneath the surface, however, thanks to the three forces that we have repeatedly seen producing fresh growth in Russian history: re-

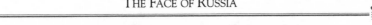

discovering the West, recovering Orthodox Christianity, and renewing links with the natural world.

This time, concern for nature was the driving force. Russians began to realize that water, the lifeblood of their landlocked empire, was being poisoned by the Soviet system. The Aral Sea was drying up because of mindless irrigation; rivers in Siberia were being polluted with waste from nuclear and biological weapon manufacture and the rivers in European Russia by the overuse of chemical fertilizers.

Defending Russian nature became the *idée fixe* of the most important new cultural phenomenon of the Brezhnev period, the so-called village writers. These conservative figures from provincial Russia were appalled by the degradation of rural life and values. They helped rally the nation to stop the pollution of the world's greatest repository of fresh water, the once pristine Lake Baikal. In the late 1980s, they made the proposed reversal of river flows in Siberia a rallying point for resistance to central planning and a reason for Russia itself to consider withdrawing from the Soviet Union.

Sympathetic scientists within the Soviet Academy of Sciences shocked the Soviet political establishment by producing in the late 1980s, on their own time, a lengthy documentary movie, *Land in Desolation*, that traced the ecological and cultural devastation of the entire Volga River basin during the Soviet era. The disastrous explosion of a nuclear reactor at Chernobyl in the spring of 1986 intensified the growing popular belief that nature itself must be defended against the unnatural schemes of the Communist elite.

The return to religion was accelerated by the popular

success in the late 1960s of Andrei Tarkovsky's film *Andrei Rublev*, which celebrated the return of bells as well as icons to Russian churches in Rublev's time after devastation by the Mongols and despite the temptations of secular paganism. The film used Eisenstein's technique of switching suddenly from black-and-white to color—but this time in order to heighten the impact of Rublev's completion of his greatest icons.

The celebration of the millennium of Russian Christianity in 1988 proved to be the most important commemorative event of the age. Footage was drawn out of archives for important documentary films that showed for the first time Stalin's blowing up of the Church of Christ the Savior in December, 1931, and the conversion of the Solovetsk Monastery in the far north into the 20th century's first death camp. The full realization grew of how much of the Russian heritage had been wantonly destroyed and how extensive had been the martyrology of Russian Christianity.

The cinema of the late Soviet period helped create an altogether new moral and spiritual atmosphere. Three giants of that era drew on different aspects of Eisenstein's artistic method to repudiate his political message and to begin the delegitimization of Communism.

Alexei German, like Eisenstein, used the black-and-white documentary form to provide fictionalized recreations of key chapters of Soviet history. But his dramas, unlike Eisenstein's, focus on ordinary people, not extraordinary leaders. Unlike the "positive heroes" and "new Soviet men" who knew no fear and had no doubts, German's more believable anti-heroes suffer in loneliness—a provincial policeman during the "building of so-

cialism" in the 1930s (*My Friend Ivan Lapshin*, 1985), a soldier on his way to Stalingrad during the war (*Twenty Days without War*, 1976), another soldier who briefly collaborated with the enemy but honestly seeks to rejoin the Russian camp (*Trial on the Road*, filmed 1971, released 1986).

Sergei Paradjanov, like Eisenstein, was a master at taking unusual images and sounds wherever he found them and rearranging them in sequences that arouse the emotions and mix eros with religion. But his best images, unlike Eisenstein's, are more surreal than real. He gradually became the Kandinsky of cinema, taking the new medium and a new generation of viewers into the cinematic *terra incognita* of abstract expressionism.

Paradjanov's montage leads us not into Eisenstein's world of applied politics, but into a reverie on pure beauty. *Shadows of Forgotten Ancestors* (1964) follows Tarkovsky in slowing down time, and uses clashing colors and jump cuts like Eisenstein's to transport us into an idealized, primordial world. Paradjanov seemed to have found his Paradise Lost not in Eisenstein's Mexico, but in a series of semi-imaginary microworlds on the periphery of Russia itself. *Shadows* is a kind of Romeo and Juliet fantasy that unfolds in an exotic, indeterminate place in the Carpathian Mountains where time seems to have stopped.

Paradjanov's life and work seem laced with paradox and suggestive of tragedy. He was imprisoned three times in the Soviet Union for deviant sex. Yet he produced in *Shadows* one of the most protracted, beautiful, and chaste scenes of a man and woman slowly and romantically coming together in ecstatic union in the entire history of the cinema. He then drew up a brilliant, 10-part scenario for a film, *Kievan Frescoes*, to commemorate the officially approved subject of the victory over Nazi Germany. He planned to mix Ukrainian images with the music of Bach and the painting of Velasquez, but he was never able to film it.

Constantly bedeviled by Soviet censors, Paradjanov dreamed of producing a film called *Confession*, which would show an ancient, historic cemetery being slowly surrounded by a new Soviet city. The Soviet officials decide to bulldoze it completely and create one of their grotesque "Parks of Culture and Rest" over it. The terrorized populace remains silent; and the ancestors, released from their graves, roam and haunt the realm that has repudiated its heritage. An epilogue was to show the majestic entry into Red Square of a giant festive parade led by Lillian Gish. Showing once again the influence of D. W. Griffith (in this case the racist element in *Birth of a Nation*), Paradjanov envisaged the film ending with that heroine of silent film ("who we always thought was mute") being suddenly hit by a mysterious black man, which causes her to begin speaking for the first time. Paradjanov sees that she is directly addressing him. "And it is just at this moment that I choose to die."

Though Paradjanov in many ways led the audio-visual renewal of Russia, he was never able to produce a film in the Russian Republic. He worked in the peripheral republics of the quietly crumbling Soviet Union. His themes were taken from the literature and folklore of Moldavia, Ukraine, the Islamic Republics, and, above all, the two ancient Christian republics of the Caucasus: the Armenia of his ancestry and Georgia, where he was born and mostly lived.

His last years were spent on a series of films designed to constitute a new kind of Caucasian film style. It was the very opposite of the realistic Soviet film filled with heroic action and assured of a happy ending. Paradjanov's hero is almost always a lonely, self-sacrificial artist. The images are largely symbolic and reminiscent of church frescoes or Persian miniatures. His purpose was "to find in the static image a global dynamic"—or what he sometimes called an "interior dynamic." He seems to have seen his films as pathways that can lead others into their own dream-like sequence of meditations on the universal questions of life and death and creativity. All this he contrasted not just with the banality of Soviet narrative films, but also with the "Niagara falls" of monotonously repetitive Western action films.

Paradjanov provided a positive hero of a totally un-Soviet type in his ultimate masterpiece, *The Color of the Pomegranate* (1970). The color is blood red; the images are either abstract or symbolic; and the hero is the great artist, monk, and martyr of Paradjanov's Armenia, Sayat-Nova.

The subject for *Pomegranate*, Paradjanov's masterpiece, was an 18th-century Armenian troubadour who also could not create his art in the country he wished to serve (Armenia). Sayat-Nova wrote his love songs in the court of the neighboring King of Georgia, became a monk, and was eventually garroted on the high altar of a Georgian cathedral by Muslim Persian invaders. His poetic legacy is, ironically, most fully preserved in the Azeri language of Muslim Azerbaijan, the bitterest current enemy of Christian Armenia in the ever-turbulent Caucasus region.

Paradjanov's depiction of the poet's martyrdom begins on top of, and then moves inside, a simple, generic cathedral. An invisible God calls out to the poet two words that are his inescapable commands: "Sing...Die." The climactic tableau is dominated by an enigmatic but beautiful Muse who continually stares at us like some archaic Goddess. The poet walks in slowly behind her dressed in simple white. He kneels and has red wine poured on him by an unidentified third person.

Earlier images in the film incline us to associate the wine with juice spilling forth from the cut pomegranate, along with the blood of Christ sacrificing himself for the sins of the world and with the bitter wine of the artist seeking truth in a world of power. One critic has suggested that the scene represents "the slow hemorrhage of a poet committing suicide." Sadly, this great work has been seen almost solely in a version that was doubly censored—first by the cultural police of the USSR and secondly by Muslim extremists in Iran through which it was first smuggled out of the USSR.

Paradjanov, like Sayat-Nova, worked and died in Georgia. And it was a Georgian movie-maker, Tengiz Abuladze, who produced the decisive cultural explosion of the late Soviet period—working with the same basic ingredients that Paradjanov had used in *The Pomegranate*: enigmatic women, a suffering artist, and a Georgian cathedral.

The small Georgian Republic gave Russia both Joseph Stalin and Lavrenty Beria, the last and most awesome chief of his secret police, the ultimate purveyor of totalitarianism. In the late years of that dying system, Georgia produced the one great artistic creation, Abuladze's *Repentance*, that, more than any other, delegitimized and ultimately helped to break up the entire Soviet system.

Abuladze was a youthful admirer of Eisenstein and wrote him a letter of appreciation after seeing *Ivan the Terrible*. Abuladze never fulfilled his early dream of studying under Eisenstein, but he came to Moscow to work in the studio of one of his most faithful disciples (and Paradjanov's collaborator on *The Pomegranate*), Sergei Yutkevich. After a long and varied career in Georgia, which had a particularly rich film tradition, he embarked in the 1960s on yet another ambitious trilogy designed to have redemptive significance for the broader society.

Part I, *Prayer*, appeared in 1968, and set out his central theme of "innocence found guilty." The trilogy began where his sometime neighbor in Tbilisi, Paradjanov, had ended: recreating the life of a great national poet (the late 19th and early 20th century Georgian bard, Vazha Pshaveli) in a bleak and timeless mountain setting. Part II, *The Tree of Desire*, appeared a decade later (1978) and moves closer to the present, telling of the search, in a pre-revolutionary Georgian village, for the legendary tree that can make dreams come true. Part III, *Repentance*, was written in 1981–82, shot in 1983–84, and finally shown in Georgia in 1986 and in Moscow in 1987.

Repentance provided a surreal picture of the real Soviet Union. It was built artistically around an explosion, and it caused one in Soviet society. A poet is pursued and persecuted by a dictator who is the composite image of Hitler, Stalin, and Beria rolled into one alternately comic and terrifying figure. The dictator is dead, but no one is able to keep him buried, and, at the moment when the poet seems about to expire from a grotesque, slow crucifixion, the film jump cuts to his terrified, grieving relatives and the deafening sound of a church being blown up. An unforgettable long scene shows a mother and daughter, unable to get any word from the gulag, searching amidst logs shipped in from Siberia for some small carved message from the Hell of high Stalinism. They seem to find familiar initials, and they huddle together stroking the log in a scene reminiscent of the icon of Our Lady of Tenderness.

The final scene in *Repentance* is one of the great moments in the history of the Russian cinema. There has been a second explosion when the young idealist shoots himself with a gun given to him by the dictator, because he found no repentance in his parents' generation which had so benefitted from the dictator. But things have quieted down, and the scene has shifted now to a thoroughly conventional couple from the Soviet new class who are comfortably feeding themselves a rich and fluffy cake that is in the shape of a church. The role of the woman carving the cake is played by the same beautiful actress who had been the Muse in the last scene of *The Color of the Pomegranate*.

Suddenly a very old woman appears at the window and asks if this is the road to the church. The young woman tells her that there no longer is a church. The old lady then quietly asks "What is the use of a road if it doesn't lead to a church?" and walks slowly down the long road.

She was, in real life, the great actress Veliko Anjaparidze, and she died just a few weeks after filming this cameo role. She was, many believe, performing her own act of repentance for the role that her husband had played as a zealous writer of Communist propaganda during the worst days of Stalinist repression.

Appearing as it did during the year when Russia was preparing to celebrate the millennium of its Christian heritage, this powerful film helped implant the idea that it was not enough to reform the system as Gorbachev was doing. There was a deeper need for spiritual closure and an altogether new beginning. The vehicle for conveying that message came to be television, to which Abuladze had turned in Tbilisi in order to put the production out of the easy reach of Moscow film censors.

The people in power who made it possible for the Russian people to see this film—first on television and later in theatres—were the two leading figures in the Gorbachev entourage who had themselves concluded that fundamental rather than just cosmetic change was needed in the USSR: Alexander Yakovlev and Eduard Shevardnadze. The latter played a particularly important role. He not only protected the project as the head of the Communist Party in Georgia, but he almost certainly did so at least in part as an act of repentance for his own prior role as head of the security forces in Georgia.

I got some hint at a state dinner in Moscow during the Reagan-Gorbachev summit in June, 1988, that Gorbachev, for all his love of discourse with intellectuals, was not personally engaged in the spiritual side of Russia's ferment. Abuladze's film was, by then, the most talked about movie in a Russia that was at the emotional and theatrical high point of its celebration of its Christian millennium. Raisa Gorbachev was getting ready for her own appearance at an enormous kitsch celebration in the Bolshoi Theatre whose ceiling was lined with church bells that were to ring at the finale. I introduced Gorbachev to Abuladze, and he evinced no sign of recogni-

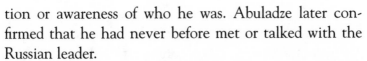

tion or awareness of who he was. Abuladze later confirmed that he had never before met or talked with the Russian leader.

As the Berlin Wall came down and Communism evaporated in eastern Europe, the 19-million-man Russian Communist Party and its entrenched bureaucratic control system began to look for ways to inoculate the multiethnic Soviet Union against the contagion of self-government. They drew blood in Georgia in April, 1989, killing peaceful demonstrators in Tbilisi, and the tension steadily mounted.

No one could be sure in the summer of 1991 that the process of reform that Mikhail Gorbachev had started would continue. The engine of change had developed more speed and momentum than anyone had expected in the five short years since he and a younger generation had assumed power. There had been so much change in the Soviet empire that the old roadmaps had to be discarded. Yet no one knew where Russia itself was headed.

Three events deepened fear among the reformers in the year leading up to the Communist coup attempt in August, 1991: the unsolved axe murder in September, 1990, of Father Alexander Men, the most powerful single force for Christian renewal among the young; the sudden resignation in December of Foreign Minister Eduard Shevardnadze, the leading reformist in the government, who warned of a coming dictatorship; and the use of armed troops to threaten Lithuania after it became the first republic to declare independence from the Soviet Union in March, 1991.

On Monday, August 19, the day before a very large degree of autonomy was to be extended to all Soviet Republics, Gorbachev's top associates announced that the vacationing Gorbachev was ill and claimed power for their junta as a massive cohort of tanks rolled into Moscow. I was an eyewitness in Moscow at the time to the process by which the Russian people rallied against the putsch. By the end of the week, they had sent the tanks back to their bases. Miraculously, the democratic resistance had made Russia rather than the USSR the legitimate unit of power and Yeltsin rather than Gorbachev their leader.

I, along with many others, have written accounts of how this astonishingly sudden, almost bloodless, and totally unexpected turnaround occurred. We still lack a vocabulary, however, to describe adequately a process that was more a meltdown than a revolution. Communist authority was, in essence, dissolved by a moral transformation from below in a time of peace and order—almost the exact opposite of the coup from above amidst war and chaos that had brought Communism to power in 1917.

Russia was experiencing yet another unexpected sudden change—one that occurred without any bombs going off or shots fired. And it precipitated yet another "Time of Troubles" in which change has been chaotic, power divided, and no authority fully legitimized in the eyes of the populace.

On the surface, the August events confirmed the results of the election of June, 1991, in the Russian Republic, which had made Boris Yeltsin the first leader chosen by universal suffrage in Russian history. After the August events, Russia resumed and accelerated its journey down the rocky road of trying to build a democratic rule of law and a market economy. In effect, Russia was seceding from the Soviet Union, and the rest of the republics were free to follow.

Deep cultural forces were at work and came to the surface during the dramatic 48 hours of August 19–20 when the outcome hung in the balance. The miscellaneous defenders that gathered around Yeltsin's White House found strength and a measure of unity by drawing—spontaneously and often sub-consciously—on two of the factors which we have consistently seen to be the driving forces behind sudden creative advances in Russian culture: their own religious heritage and the latest Western ideas. Both of these forces had been suppressed by Communism. The way in which they are either brought into harmony or allowed to generate conflict could well determine how and when—perhaps even if—Russia will finally emerge from its post-Communist troubles and move on to fresh achievement.

Religious categories subliminally suggested to the uninformed and largely uncommitted masses on the very first day of the coup attempt that this was a case of bad guys attacking good guys. The Communist junta had imposed a news blackout and assumed that their massive show of force in Moscow would convince everyone that their cause was unstoppable. Their only public appearance was a claustrophobic, indoor televised press conference centered on the leader of the coup, Gennady Yanaev. He appeared with shaded eyeglasses, shifting eyes, and shaking hands. The contrast was almost total with the only picture everyone had of the opposition: a white-haired, smiling Yeltsin climbing on a tank in the outdoors and raising a confident fist. In a culture that had debased the meaning of words and on a day when no one was sure what was really going on, Russians sensed from visual images who was good and who was bad.

An unusual mix of people who had suffered under the Soviet system joined the young people in the human wall defending Yeltsin's White House: Afghan veterans, Siberian visitors to Moscow, a few young priests, and—most important and least reported of all—long-suffering older women. Long ignored or patronizingly dismissed by Soviet and Western commentators alike as "old women in church," they played a key role in rebuking and morally disarming the young soldiers in the tanks. In the absence of clear commands from on high, those on the front lines were suddenly subjected to an alternative line of command: their mothers.

Almost all the quarreling forces that came into—and began fighting over—power came from this resistance, and looked in part to the Russian Orthodox Church for added legitimation and mediation. Then and since, Russians were rediscovering in fragmentary ways long-buried and dimly understood, but newly relevant Judaeo-Christian ideas: the redemptive value of unmerited suffering, the necessity of moral choice, the individual's responsibility to a higher authority than the state, and the continued possibility of miracles. Some, though not many, recognized an obligation and need for repentance.

The overthrow of the Soviet system could probably not have occurred as rapidly, peacefully, and decisively as it did without the widespread feeling that Russia was recovering its deeper self in the process. This was made particularly evident in the immediate heroic accounts that Russian television gave of the events as soon as it went back on the air. The three young men who had been accidentally killed summoned up memories of the first Russian saints, Boris and Gleb, who had accepted voluntary death in order to bring Rus back together; hand sketches of St. George slaying the Dragon had been widely brandished in the human wall around the White House; and the whiteness of the building and of Yeltsin's hair was for a brief moment blended into images of the "white-stoned" Moscow of the medieval chronicles and the white-haired hero-saints of iconography. A new mythology seemed to be in the making through the new medium of the masses: television.

Televised images, not words, had inspired the resistance. The two most decisive actions were Yeltsin's mounting the tank and the forming of a human wall around him thereafter. These events did not occur in response to words that had been uttered, but were shaped subliminally by images that had been seen—of the boy in Tiananmen Square who stopped the tank and of the Lithuanians who had formed a similar circle around their government building in response to a similar threat.

The resistance could not be atomized or cut off from the outside world, because the young people were armed with faxes, e-mail, portable phones, and CNN. Visual images of life in the West undermined volumes of negative Soviet propaganda and fed the appetite for change.

Rediscovery of the West, therefore, was the decisive factor behind the great transformation of power. Gorbachev's *perestroika* (reconstruction) had been largely a Leninist slogan for managing change without relinquishing control. But *glasnost* (openness, being able to speak up) was a reality; and a new, better-educated, post-war, post-Stalinist generation vaguely wanted to experience the freedoms and possibilities for greater prosperity that most Russians now realized that Western societies had produced in the post-war era.

After another long period of cultural isolation under authoritarian rule, Russians were now looking to the West—as they had under Catherine the Great and Alexander II—not just for ideas but for models. In part they were replicating the recurrent Russian tendency to take their main model for a new creative enterprise from precisely their principal Western adversary.

The United States, which the Soviet Union had for so long seen as its main enemy, had nonetheless been the model that Russians secretly studied and publicly sought to "overtake and surpass." After the failed Communist coup and the subsequent dissolution of the Soviet Union in late 1991, the new Russian leadership looked to America more broadly not just as a model but as a potential partner in their own new effort to build a representative, federal democracy in a multi-cultural society on a continental scale.

The American response was cordial at the high political level and often generous at the popular level. But America as a nation did not seem able either to engage imaginatively in their experiment in building a free democracy or to invest much substantively in opening up for development the world's greatest supply of untouched natural resources. The Russians, who had themselves overthrown Communism, believed they had done something big (*podvig*, meaning heroic deed). They thought Americans also thought big, but increasingly came to feel that America in particular and the West in general were responding only with *malye dela* (small deeds). The center of political gravity steadily moved in an authoritarian, nationalist direction. The drastic decline in state support for all aspects of culture caused many highly educated people to become nostalgic for the more secure if less free conditions that they enjoyed in a more controlled and chauvinistic Russia.

Yeltsin himself ordered the White House shelled when it became the base for his nationalist opposition. He was elected again in 1996, but his popularity waned. Boris Yeltsin like Boris Godunov was trying to reform Russia, but no one could be sure how long Russia's new "Time of Troubles" would last—or how it would end.

The crucial question for the future—in terms of the cultural pattern we have been tracing—is simply this: Will post-Soviet Russia end up, after its initial period of wholesale adaptation of Western models, with its own original and sustainable form of an open and accountable society? Or will that effort break up—and Russia move on to establish yet another form of the autocratic and closed society that has dominated so much of its past history?

In terms of the bearers of culture we have been discussing, the question now is what social group and what medium of expression will most shape that future? The Communist Revolution of 1917 destroyed both the monastic and the aristocratic elites that had successively dominated earlier Russian culture. The recent transformation and opening up of Russia to market forces has largely destroyed the new Communist elite that replaced all earlier ones and layered a vast security machine on top of the inherited state bureaucracy to create a kind of anti-culture. The post-Soviet advent of openness and commercialism has also largely destroyed the Russian intelligentsia. That cosmopolitan, urbanized elite, which had historically opposed both Tsarist and Communist authority, neither created nor benefitted from the great transformation of 1991.

The turnaround represented—for the first time in Russian history—peaceful political change directly imposed by a broadly representative popular movement, rather than by a small elite. It was the spontaneous improvisation of many different people with different interests. Only slowly did a new "elite" begin to emerge, as the younger generation particularly in the provinces began to gain experience in the wide range of professions from which the new Russia seemed to be increasingly recruiting its leaders. But what could be the new art form, if Russia's experiment in democracy and a market economy should succeed?

The new electronic media seemed likely to play a part in a nation with high technological literacy that was entering the information age. The coup attempt of August 1991 had been well planned and succeeded in gaining control of the traditional "commanding heights" of communication that Communist tacticians had written about: telegraph stations, newspaper offices, and even television stations. But in the age of photocopying machines and instant electronic communication, the young people resisting the coup often had better communication with the outside world than those trying to execute the coup had even with each other.

Television, as we have noted, engraved in the public a heroic, even epic image of the August days, and the advancing Internet has since brought the Russian people more and more information from the outside world. But the medium itself was becoming in many ways the message, and the message seemed at times to be the total westernization and commercialization of everything.

If the cinema was almost forced out of business by the loss of its government subsidy, the new form of moving pictures, television, was prospering. Its most artistic product seemed to be animated satire such as *Kukli* (Puppets), a popular series that caricatures with genuine humor the entire political establishment. A journal of the Yeltsin government announced in 1996 a national contest for defining a positive ideology for the new Russia, and Yeltsin himself appointed a commission to draw one up. Many found it encouraging that neither effort succeeded in doing more than drawing up a laundry list of platitudes.

Early in 1998 in Moscow, I asked Gregory Satarov, the bright young former top aid to Yeltsin who had headed the commission, to give me his own view of where Russia would find its future identity amidst all the current confusion. He described a recent episode in another often satirical series on Russian television: *Tales of the New Russia*. In a very brief sequence—more the length of an advertisement than of a segment in a TV drama—the tale shows a young child trying to build a house with blocks while his parents are quarreling. They pursue one another furiously from room to room, sneezing, as wind and rain blow in from an open window. They eventually knock over the building that the industrious, silent child has been putting together. He looks up and in a quiet voice asks them please just to shut the window. They do so and begin repairing the house they all live in.

It is as good an image as one is likely to find of the unspoken but growing hope in Russia that a new generation will in time be able quietly to build a new Russia and move beyond the familial bloodletting of the past and the present chaotic time of transition. That hope is most likely to be fulfilled if Russians can at last find a way of life that will accommodate all three of the passions that have made them creative: the desire to borrow the material accomplishments of others, to draw on their own spiritual heritage, and to keep alive their links with the natural world.

Conclusion

We have looked at the history of the Russian people by focusing on the anguish, achievements, and aspirations of a few great artists. I have seen it to be a culture of explosive revolution rather than gradual evolution. I have suggested that different art media successively rose to special greatness and historical importance in particular ages. I have tried to suggest some ways in which each art form successively impacted on Russian culture—and how each went through a three-stage process that begins with total imitation, reaches its zenith through radical innovation, and finally breaks down because of metaphysical overload from above—or breaks up because of social unrest from below.

I have left untouched the technical side of each art form; and left out many great artists and forms of artistic expression about which an even richer tale might well be told. There would probably be a greater consensus among cognoscenti for focusing, for instance, on the scientist and polymath Mikhail Lomonosov instead of Rastrelli and the classical perfection of Pavlovsk rather than the baroque grandeur of Tsarskoe Selo for the 18th century; on Pushkin rather than Gogol for literature in the early 19th; on Tchaikovsky rather than Musorgsky and on ballet rather than opera for the late 19th; and on literature rather than cinema for the 20th. And, in stressing the religious base to Russian culture, I could have given some attention to sectarian (and more recently Baptist and Pentecostal) spirituality and not just focused on the historic Orthodox tradition.

I deliberately chose, however, figures and forms that seemed to express something generally thought to be deeply and distinctively Russian—and different from the mainstream experience of culture in the West. I do not pretend to have plumbed the depths of the Russian soul, but I have tried to look hard at some unfamiliar contours on the body.

The body turns out to have features that I had not initially expected. All of the key figures among the very deeply Russian artists featured in this narrative also had roots in other cultures. Rublev worked closely with Greeks and South Slavs; Rastrelli was Italian; Gogol, Ukrainian; Musorgsky, part Tatar; Eisenstein, part Jewish; Paradjanov, Armenian; Abuladze, Georgian.

The great 91-year-old sage of St. Petersburg, Dmitry Likhachev, has brilliantly shown in his late writings the extent to which Russia has always had a far more absorbent culture and multi-ethnic population than has been generally recognized. As the greatest living student of Russian culture, he has become its living memory. He is what the native peoples of America sometimes called the wisest old man of the tribe—"the dream keeper."

Likhachev is also in many ways the conscience of Russia—having survived the 20th century's first death camp at Solovetsk and an attempt on his life after he had spoken up against expelling and exiling the great human rights activist, Andrei Sakharov, from the Academy of Sciences. He was saved from the stabbing, providentially, by a manuscript within his coat. Likhachev was a witness in Petersburg to the Communist takeover in 1917 and a force for its demise in August, 1991. When the outcome of the Communist putsch was uncertain and the future of Russia hung in the balance, he spoke out eloquently in front of the Winter Palace and, in effect, helped to close the circle, which brought a peaceful end to the age of violence and utopian revolutions.

When I asked Likhachev recently why so many of the great works of Russian art remained unfinished even in peaceful times, he reflected that what was important for many great figures in Russian culture was not completing their work so much as exploring the process of creation. It seems to me that Russians often expect that their stories will somehow flow into our lives—and that the ending may bring us all together, perhaps in another life altogether.

I could have tried plunging into the psychological labyrinths of the artists' lives, but it seemed important to do so only in the case of Eisenstein, because he alone reflected on and wrote about that dimension. Humanistic history, it seems to me, has a special obligation to reflect and respect distinctive modes of thought from the past—and not lightly to superimpose on the fragmentary record categories and modes of thought from other ages.

Nor did it seem necessary to itemize the elements of anti-Semitism, anti-Catholicism, and other forms of prejudice that are at times detectable even in great figures like Gogol and Musorgsky. These attitudes are not central to their art—but are central to the authoritarian mentality that has feared and censored art throughout most of Russian history. This chauvinistic anti-culture threatens Russia even today and deserves thorough study in an altogether different kind of book. Likhachev distinguishes nationalism, which is fueled by negative hatred towards foreign and internal enemies, from patriotism, which grows out of positive pride in one's own people and culture.

I would like to have discussed two of my own favorite forms of Russian prose—the more familiar and accessible novellas of Turgenev and plays of Chekhov—and the Russian theme of "family happiness" which neither Gogol nor Musorgsky nor Eisenstein enjoyed during their adult years. But intense and historically important artistic creativity is often the work of lonely people whose lives are far from normal. Musorgsky may have made the best diagnosis of his own recurring mental illness when he wrote early in life that "my soul has killed my body." Surely, the broken bodies and the incomplete bodies of work left behind by artists like Gogol and Musorgsky and Eisenstein have helped restore the soul—not just of Russians, but of anyone anywhere who becomes immersed in what they were trying to achieve.

In recent times, Russian cinema and other aspects of Russian culture have been threatened with near-extinction by the commercialism and influx of pulp culture from abroad. But both artistic quality and moral force have been maintained in new films like Sergei Bobrov's *Prisoner of the Mountains* (1996) and Alexei German's *Khrustalev, Get the Car* (1998). Both films deal deeply and directly with key problems of contemporary Russia: the former with the tragedy of Russia's war in Chechnya, the latter with Russia's continued attempt to understand what really happened in the last days of Stalin. Both films rise above the simple heroes-

and-villains plots of the past, and show that there is good and bad in everyone. These films do not preach, but suggest dramatically the need to move on to a new type of society in which moral categories and individual responsibility can again have meaning.

Dmitry Likhachev has seen it all. When I last talked with him in March, 1998, in Petersburg, he was hopeful for the future. The new generation was taking hold both politically and culturally in the provinces, and people were sending him a growing number of studies documenting and talking through the martyrology of Russian culture at the grassroots level. Russian culture was no longer just the product of an elite, whether monastic, aristocratic, intellectual, or political. As I left him, the waiters in the hotel were lining up to get his autograph.

The most serious omission from this narrative is poetry, which has been one of the greatest and most popular ways in which Russians have talked with themselves and reached for the stars ever since Pushkin exploded on the scene at the dawn of the 19th century.

Russia produced probably the greatest constellation of poets anywhere in the world in the first three decades of the 20th century. Russian poetry in this "silver age" was written in a wide variety of experimental styles (acmeism, futurism, symbolism, imaginism) by people from an equally wide variety of ethnic and regional backgrounds. Poetry like the other arts took to the stage in the late imperial and early Soviet periods through plays in verse and recitations accompanied by guitar or balalaika. Later generations hearkened to the attenuated echo of Mayakovsky at histrionic public readings of mildly dissident new verse before large audiences. Readings by poets like Evgeny Evtushenko and Andrei Voznesensky became important cultural phenomena in the 1960s and 1970s, helping to compensate for the absence of either legalized political opposition or good live entertainment in the "years of stagnation."

The greatest poets of the Soviet era—Osip Mandelstam, Anna Akhmatova, Boris Pasternak, and Joseph Brodsky—suffered physically, yet gave Russians spiritual compensation at a deeper level. Through the magic of language, they provided a moral alternative not just to the cruelty, but to the banality of Soviet totalitarianism. In the USSR prose was debased into propaganda and ordinary speech into acronyms and exhortation. Poetry helped people talk and think on a higher level. It enabled young Russians to look back and beyond "the generation that killed its poets" and hear again richer voices from the past. The most powerful reading and reciting of Russian poetry occurred not in amphitheaters on state-sponsored "days of poetry." It occurred within families and small groups of friends, where human warmth and honesty could be preserved against the coldness and falsehood that prevailed outside.

Poetry brought women into the mainstream of Russian culture for the first time since the reign of the great empresses of the 18th century. Marina Tsvetaeva was one of the best—and one of the many suicides. The last great lady of pre-revolutionary, aristocratic Petersburg, Anna Akhmatova, wrote two elegiac epics that were, in their own way, as magnificent as Rastrelli palaces: *Poem without a Hero* and *Requiem*. In the terse prose preface to the latter poem, she recalls waiting endlessly in a dehumanizing line at the worst time of terror and privation under

Stalin. Another woman asks her in a whisper if anyone could ever describe this scene. Akhmatova replied "'I can.' And something like a smile passed briefly over what had once been her face."

One of the great moments of truth on the Soviet stage in the Brezhnev years came in the climactic scene of the Taganka Theatre production of Brecht's *Galileo*. The great scientist, played by the most popular poet-folksinger of the age, Vladimir Vysotsky, has just recanted his life's work before the Inquisition, and his youthful, idealistic follower is disconsolate. "Cursed be the land," he sobs, "that must live without heroes." Vysotsky (who died shortly thereafter at age 42, like Gogol and Musorgsky) slowly turns around, and his craggy, alcohol-ridden face looks at and beyond the hushed audience as he replies quietly: "Cursed be the land that always has need of heroes."

Poets helped lift the curse and build new bridges. Two of Jewish extraction, Pasternak and Brodsky, found words that gave new meaning to old icons—and wrote two of the most powerful Christian poems of the 20th century.

Gogol and Musorgsky in the relatively peaceful 19th century had been obsessed with death and darkness. Pasternak in the midst of the turbulent and bloody 20th century writes of resurrection in the last poetic lines of *Doctor Zhivago*. The title summons up images of the icon that shows Jesus, risen from the dead, looking back to the women by the tomb, and asking "Why seek ye the living (*zhivago*) amidst the dead?" The verse suggests that history is not some impersonal force, but rather a "parable" in which artists must suffer, but miracles are possible.

I descend into the grave, and on the third day, rise.
And, like barks weaving down a river,
The centuries shall come like a caravan of barges
Into judgment, to me, out of darkness.

Brodsky lived later but died younger than Pasternak. He never returned to Russia after his expulsion in 1972. He lived on to write beautifully in English as well as Russian—and even to force volumes of poetry into supermarkets while serving as Poet Laureate of the United States at the Library of Congress in 1991–92, the year of Communism's collapse in Russia. Thanks to a Russian-American, the spiritual culture of poetry began to seep into the citadels of American commercialism at precisely the time the material culture of America was beginning to flood into Russia.

One of Brodsky's greatest poems sheds new light on the old and relatively neglected icon of Christ's Presentation in the Temple. Instead of focusing on the Virgin Mary, he writes about her mother, whom he identifies with Anna Akhmatova by calling her "the Prophetess Anna" rather than simply Anne. And he gives center stage to the old Jew Simeon who holds up the newborn baby:

to light up the path that leads into death's realm
where never before until this point in time
had any man managed to lighten a path.
The old man's torch glowed.
And the pathway widened.

Poetry more than any other art form kept faces human

throughout Russia's terrible 20th century, from Pasternak to Brodsky. It was around the stove in the kitchen of Mandelstam's widow during the winter of 1966–67 that I began to sense the beginning of Russia's renewal. A continuous flow of remarkable people came to participate in evenings presided over by her, whose husband had died in the gulag, and Varlam Shalamov, the great writer who had somehow survived the most remote death camp at Kolyma (see illustration 30). The sense of renewal came not just from young men, but also from the old women who had lived on—women like the wife of her brother, Elena Fradkina, who had finally, four years earlier, been able to recover for the first time the experimental art of her youth. At the moving opening of the first exhibit she had ever been able to hold of the sets she had designed for the Tairov Theatre decades ago, she was asked how old she was and simply replied "four" (see illustration 31). I thought then of Gogol's last words: "Except ye become as a little child..."

Mandelstam's widow was named Nadezhda, which is the Russian word for hope. But hope seemed to wane as she moved from the first volume of her memoirs, *Hope Against Hope*, to the second volume *Hope Abandoned*. I thought I met her again, however, when I stood alongside a woman who had been part of the human wall for 48 hours in August, 1991, and was now watching the tanks drive away covered with flowers. "We always had faith and love," she quietly said. "Now we have hope."

No one can say that hope is enough, that the young will remember, that the return to Christianity will be more than a passing fad, that deep culture can survive shallow consumerism, or that democracy will ultimately prevail against authoritarianism.

The Marquis de Custine, the most brilliant observer of 19th-century Russian autocracy, noted that the Tsar "has many masks but no face." Russians today have many faces and fewer masks. They are looking back at the faces on the icons, but also looking forward to facing a different future. And, in the uncertain present, they are, as one young Russian recently put it to me, "now, at last, able to look at ourselves in a mirror."

The great square outside the Tsar's palace in Petersburg is no longer filled with either soldiers or revolutionaries. Russia's children for the 21st century can sometimes be seen frolicking there on a bouncing rubber model of Rastrelli's masterpiece. "Storming the Winter Palace" is now the name of a children's game.

As a post-Soviet generation of leaders moves closer to power, Russians seem likely to resolve their prolonged crises of legitimacy in one of two ways. They could revert once again to a centralized, xenophobic authoritarianism—probably not so much a classical "Oriental despotism" as some new variation of the European fascisms that arise out of failed democratic experiments. Or Russia could become integrated into European civilization—a continent-wide, multiethnic federation that would be, in effect, an idiosyncratic variant of the United States.

There may be no important geopolitical question today than whether or not Russia is able to produce a stable society that is both free and responsible in the heart of the Eurasian landmass. Hunger and humiliation may lead Russians to rebuild central despotic power on the basis of Russia's bureaucracy and military, those enduring forces that have always been the foes of culture. But culture itself may help impel Russian society toward a freer future.

While many great Russian artists never completed their greatest works, the creative process and moral passion underlying their strivings continue to flow into the lives of ordinary Russians. These sources of inner strength give hope that Russia may succeed in producing not only the "normal" society about which Russia's modernizing reformers speak, but also the "abnormal" new art forms that a postmodern world seems to seek.

Bibliography

I include here the works generally relied on for facts and citations used in this work as well as a few other studies that are accessible and recommended for further general reading. Works in Russian and other languages are included only if they significantly add to what is available in English.

Another volume will be published subsequently to provide full bibliographical references and summary discussions of the many controversies involved both in this particular distillation of Russian history and in the general use of artistic material for understanding the broader concerns of a people.

My own prior writings: *The Icon and the Axe. An Interpretive History of Russian Culture*, New York, 1966; "The Spirit of Russian Art," in *The Horizon Book of the Arts of Russia*, New York, 1970, pp. 7–31; *Fire in the Minds of Men*, New York, 1980; *Russia Transformed. Breakthrough to Hope, August, 1991*, New York, 1992; "The Poet Who Proved the Power of Words," *The Washington Post*, January 30, 1996, pp. D1, D3.

General Reference: F.A. Brokgauz, and I.A. Efron, *Entsiklopedichesky Slovar*, St. Petersburg, 1890–1907, 82 vols. plus 4 supplementary vols. This is still the most comprehensive and dependable Russian encyclopedia in most historical areas where it has not been superseded by new findings.

Also, Mikhail Florinsky, ed., *Encyclopedia of Russia and the Soviet Union*, New York, 1961, with information brought up to

date in *The New Encyclopedia Britannica*, Chicago, 1990, 29 vols., 15th edition. For general history, Nicholas Riasanovsky, *A History of Russia*, Oxford, 1993.

Among Soviet encyclopedias, V.M. Friche and A.V. Lunacharsky, successive editors, *Literaturnaya Entsiklopediya*. Moscow, 1930–39, vols. 1–9, 11, for modern Russian literature; Dmitry Likhachev, *The Great Heritage. The Classical Literature of Old Russia*, Moscow, 1981, for older literature. Among Russian Orthodox Church publications, *Nastolnaia kniga sviashchenosluzhitelia*, Moscow, 6 vols, esp. vol. 4, 1983; Georges Florovsky, *Ways of Russian Theology*, Belmont, Mass., 1979, 2 vols.; George Fedotov, *The Russian Religious Mind*, Cambridge, Mass., 1966, 2 vols.

On the audio-visual arts, George Hamilton, *The Art and Architecture of Russia*, London, 1954; Igor Grabar, *Istoriia Russkogo Iskusstva*, Moscow, 1910–15, 6 vols.; N.I. Brunov et al., *Istoriia Russkoi Arkhitektury*, Moscow, 1956, 2d rev. and exp. ed.; William Brumfield, *A History of Russian Architecture*, Cambridge, 1993; Camilla Gray, *The Russian Experiment in Art: 1863–1922*, London, 1962; T. Livanova, M. Pekelis, T. Popova, *Istoriia Russkoi Muzyki*, Moscow-Leningrad, 1940, 2 vols.; Abram Gozenpud, *Operny Slovar*, Moscow-Leningrad, 1965; Jay Leyda, *Kino: A History of the Russian and Soviet Film*, New York, 1973; and, for the late Soviet period, Anna Lawton, *Kinoglasnost: Soviet Cinema in Our Time*, Cambridge, 1992.

Chapter 1: Aleksandra Kostsova, *The Subjects of Early Icons*, St. Petersburg, 1991; Nicholas Kondakov, *The Russian Icon*, Oxford, 1927 (condensed from his *Russkaia Ikona*, Prague, 1928–33, 4 vols.); Leonid Uspensky and V. Lossky, *The Meaning of Icons*, Boston, 1952; L. Uspensky, *The Theology of Icons*, Crestwood, New York, 1976; Kurt Weitzmann, *The Monastery of Saint*

Catherine at Mount Sinai. The Icons, Princeton, 1976; Ekdotiki Athenon, *The Mysterious Fayum Portraits. Faces from Ancient Egypt*, London, 1995; Nathalie Labreque-Pervouchine, *L'Iconostase, une Evolution Historique en Russie*, Montreal, 1982; Boris Uspensky, *The Semiotics of the Russian Icon*, Lisse, 1976; Dmitry Likhachev, *Kultura Rusi vremeni Andreia Rubleva*, Moscow-Leningrad, 1962; V.N. Sergeev, *Rublev*, Moscow, 1981; G.I. Vzdornov, collector, *Troitsa Andreia Rubleva. Antologiia*, Moscow, 1989; A.V. Voloshinov, *Troitsa Andreia Rubleva: geometriia i filosofiia*, Saratov, 1997; Irina Danilova, *Freski Ferapontova Monastyria*, Moscow, n.d., with English text; Edward Williams, *The Bells of Russia, History and Technology*, Princeton, 1985.

Chapter 2: Alexander Opolovnikov and Yelena Opolovnikova, *The Wooden Architecture of Russia*, New York, 1989; A. Matveev, *Rastrelli*, Moscow, 1938; David Arkin, *Rastrelli*, Moscow, 1954; Dmitry Shvidkovsky, *St. Petersburg, Architecture of the Tsars*, New York, 1996; T.V. Alekseeva, ed., *Russkoe Iskusstvo Barokko.*, Moscow, 1977; B.V. Piotrovsky, ed., *Ermitazh. Istoriia Stroitelstva i Arkhitektura Zdanii*, Leningrad, 1989; *Alexander Witberg (1787–1835)*, Stockholm (Konstakademien exhibit catalogue), 1993–94; T.A. Slavina, *Konstantin Ton*, Leningrad, 1989; O.A. Chekanova, A.L. Potach, *Ogiust Monferran*, Leningrad, 1990; Tatyana Khalturina, *Gradostroitelnye Printsipy Russkogo Barokko serediny XVIII veka*, Moscow, 1984 (unpublished dissertation); N.P. Antsiferov, *Pushkin v Tsarskom Sele*, Leningrad, 1929; Dmitry Likhachev, *Poeziia Sadov*, St. Petersburg, 1991; Grigory Kaganov, *Images of Space. St. Petersburg in the Visual and Verbal Arts*, Stanford, 1997.

Chapter 3: Nicholas Gogol, *The Collected Tales and Plays of Nikolai Gogol* (tr. C. Garnett, rev. L. Kent), New York, 1964;

Dead Souls (tr. R. Pevear and L. Volokhonsky), New York, 1996; *Dukhovnaia Proza*, Moscow, 1992; Victor Erlich, *Gogol*, New Haven, 1969; Donald Fanger, *The Creation of Nikolai Gogol*, Cambridge, Mass., 1979; Leon Stillman, *Gogol*, Tenafly, N.J. 1990; David Magarshack, *Gogol. A Life*, London, 1957; Andrei Siniavsky, *V Teni Gogolia*, Paris, 1975; N. Mashkovtsev, *Gogol v Krugu Khudozhnikov*, Moscow, 1955; Yury Lotman, *V Shkole Poeticheskogo Slova: Pushkin, Lermontov, Gogol*, Moscow, 1988; Mikhail Botkin, *Aleksandr Andreevich Ivanov. Ego zhizn i perepiska 1806-1856*. St. Petersburg, 1880; Vahan Barooshian, *The Art of Liberation: Alexander A. Ivanov*, Lanham, Md., 1987.

Chapter 4: M.D. Calvocoressi, *Mussorgsky*, New York, 1962; Richard Taruskin, *Musorgsky: Eight Essays and an Epilogue*, Princeton, 1993; and his *Opera and Drama in Russia as Preached and Practiced in the 1860s*, Rochester, 1981; Jay Leyda and Sergei Bertensson, *The Musorgsky Reader. A Life of Modeste Petrovich Musorgsky in Letters and Documents*, New York, 1947; E. Levasheva, ed., *Modest Musorgsky's Heritage. Collection of Materials. To the Publication of Modest Musorgsky's Complete Works in Thirty Two Volumes*, Moscow, 1989, with text also in English; E.M. Gordeeva, *Kompozitory "Moguchei Kuchki"*, Moscow, 1986, and her *M.P. Musorgsky v Vospominaniiakh Sovremennikov*, Moscow, 1989; Tatyana Antipova, *Muzyka i Bytie*, Moscow, 1997; Nicholas Rimsky-Korsakov, *My Musical Life*, New York, 1935; G. Kiselev, *M.A. Balakirev*, Moscow, 1935; Harlowe Robinson, *Sergei Prokofiev*, New York, 1987; Elizabeth Wilson, *Shostakovich, a Life Remembered*, Princeton, 1994.

Chapter 5: Marie Seton, *Eisenstein*, London, 1978, rev. ed.; David Broadwell, *The Cinema of Eisenstein*, Cambridge, Mass., 1993; Ronald Bergen, *Eisenstein: A Life in Conflict*, London,

1997; Ivor Montagu, *With Eisenstein in Hollywood*, New York, 1967; Inga Karetnikova, *Mexico According to Eisenstein*, Albuquerque, N.M., 1991; Richard Taylor, ed., *Beyond the Stars: The Memoirs of Sergei Eisenstein*, Calcutta, 1995; Eisenstein, *Memuary*, Moscow, 1997, 2 vols.; Wiktor Woroszylski, *The Life of Mayakovski*, New York, 1970; Edward Braun, *Meyerhold, A Revolution in the Theatre*, Iowa City, 1995; Alma Law and Mel Gordon, *Meyerhold, Eisenstein and Biomechanics*, Jefferson, N.C., 1996; A.A. Mikhailova, et al., *Meierkhold i khudozhniki*, Moscow, 1995, album text also in English; V.V. Ivanov, *Ocherki po Istorii Semiotiki v SSSR*, Moscow, 1976; E.A. Speranskaia, ed., *Agitatsionno-Massovoe Iskusstvo pervykh let Oktiabra*, Moscow, 1971.

Chapter 6: Patrick Cazals, *Serguei Paradjanov*, Paris, 1993; Levon Grigorian, *Tri Tsveta Odnoi Strasti: Triptikh Sergeia Paradjanov*, Moscow, 1991; Yury Lotman, *Kultura i Vzryv*, Moscow, 1992; Dmitry Likhachev, *Reflections on Russia*, Boulder, Colo., 1991; *Vospominaniia*, St. Petersburg, 1995; Kathleen Parthé, *Russian Village Prose: The Radiant Past*, Princeton, 1992; Vladimir Zviglyanich, *The Morphology of Russian Mentality*, Lewiston, New York, 1993. Gregory Satarov, ed., *Rossiia v poiskakh idei. Analiz Pressy*, Moscow, 1997.

Index

About the Author

J AMES H. BILLINGTON has served since 1987 as the thirteenth Librarian of Congress of the United States. A Rhodes scholar at Oxford, he taught modern history with a special focus on Russian culture at Harvard and Princeton Universities from 1957 to 1973. He was Director of the Woodrow Wilson International Center for Scholars in Washington, D.C., from 1973 to 1987. Dr. Billington is the author of the classic *The Icon and the Axe: An Interpretive History of Russian Culture*, *Fire in the Minds of Men: Origins of the Revolutionary Faith*, and *Russia Transformed: Breakthrough to Hope*, an eyewitness account of the failed Communist coup in 1991 and the emergence of Russia as a democratic nation. He is one of the world's leading experts on Russia and has been a policy advisor to Presidents and Congressmen as well as leaders in the academic, ecclesiastical, and private sectors.